Dongsan Library Old Books Translation Series No. 7
English Translation Series No. 2

Travel Log of the Celestial Envoys (*Ch'ŏnsa illo ilgi*) An annotated translation

Travel Log of the Celestial Envoys
(Ch'ŏnsa illo ilgi)
An annotated translation

Printed	2024. 01. 17.
Published	2024. 01. 31.

Translator	Joshua Van Lieu
Editor	Lee Jonghan
Publisher	Synn Ilhi
Published by	Keimyung University Press Room 105, Bosangwan, Keimyung University 1095 Dalgubeol-daero, Dalseo-gu, Daegu 42601 TEL. +82-53-580-6233 FAX. +82-53-580-6235 Homepage: www.kmupress.com
Registration	1970. 9. 1. (#347-1998-1)

ISBN 979-11-6516-196-5 93910 Price ₩20,000

This book has been published with the support of the University Innovation Support Project for the 2023 academic year administered by the Ministry of Education of the Republic of Korea and the National Research Foundation of Korea.

Dongsan Library Old Books Translation Series No. 7
English Translation Series No. 2

Travel Log of the Celestial Envoys *(Ch'ŏnsa illo ilgi)* An annotated translation

Translated by Joshua Van Lieu
Edited by Lee Jonghan

KEIMYUNG UNIVERSITY PRESS

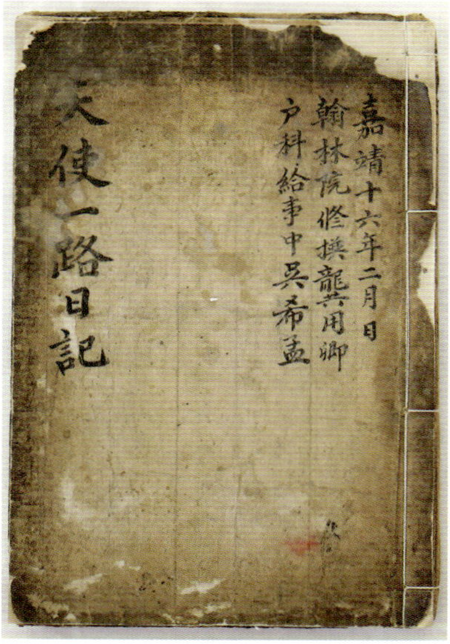

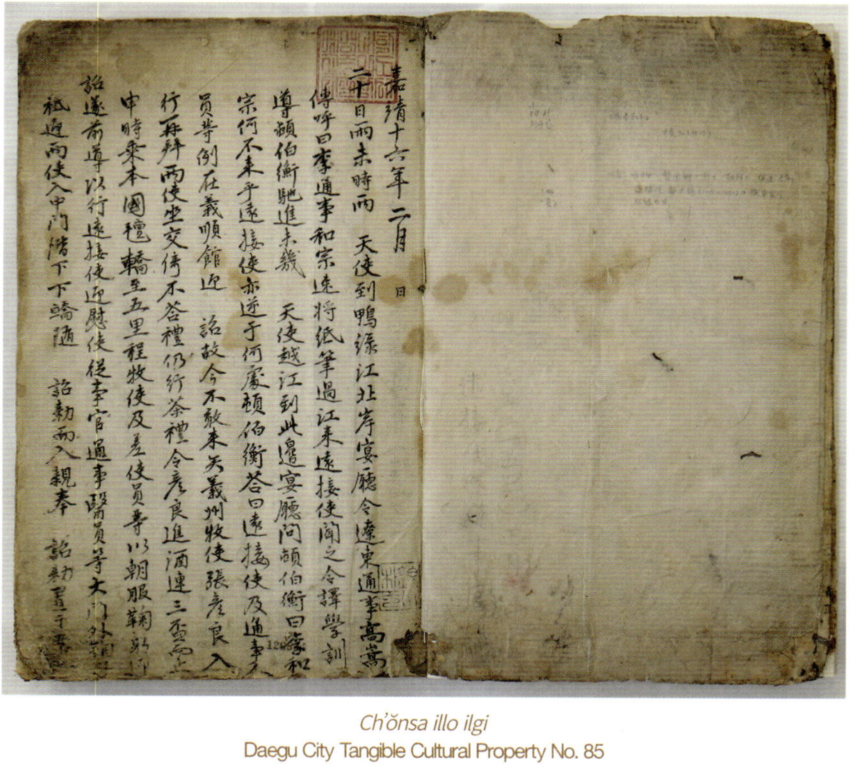

Ch'ŏnsa illo ilgi
Daegu City Tangible Cultural Property No. 85
Keimyung University Dongsan Library collection

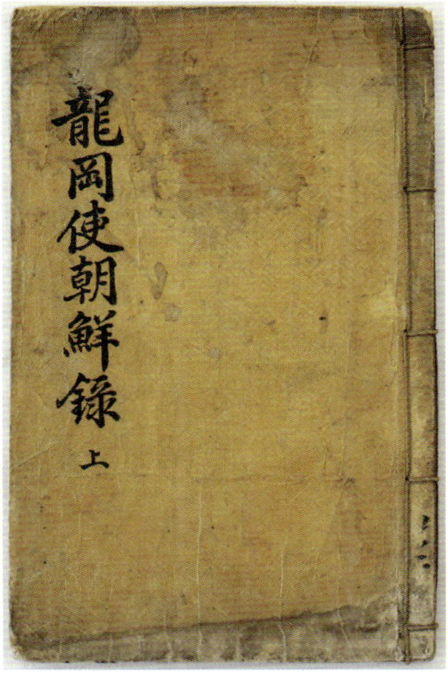

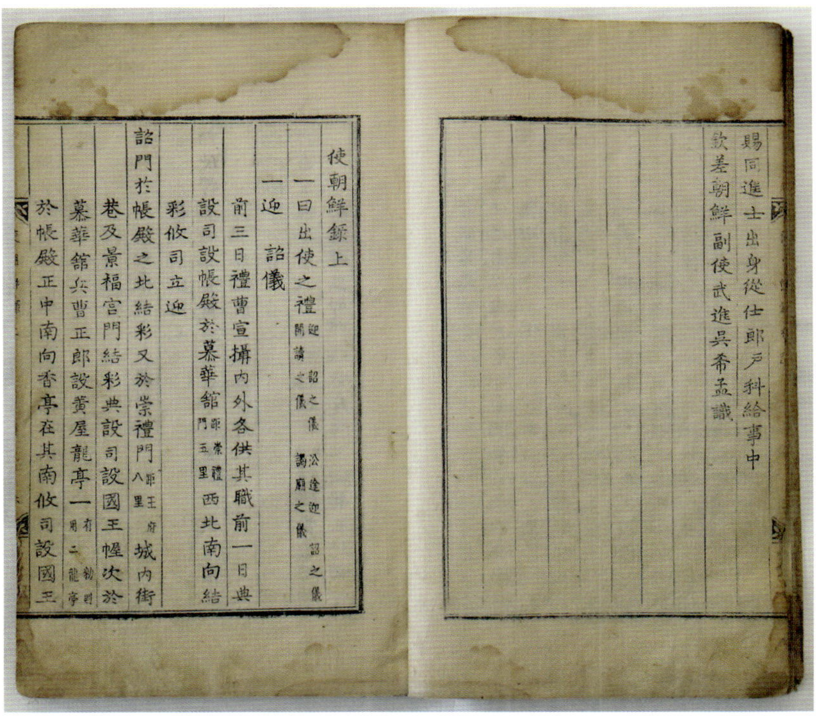

Shi chaoxian lu

A record of the Ming embassy to Chosŏn compiled by the chief Ming envoy Gong Yongqing upon his return.
Daegu City Tangible Cultural Property No. 86, Keimyung University Dongsan Library collection

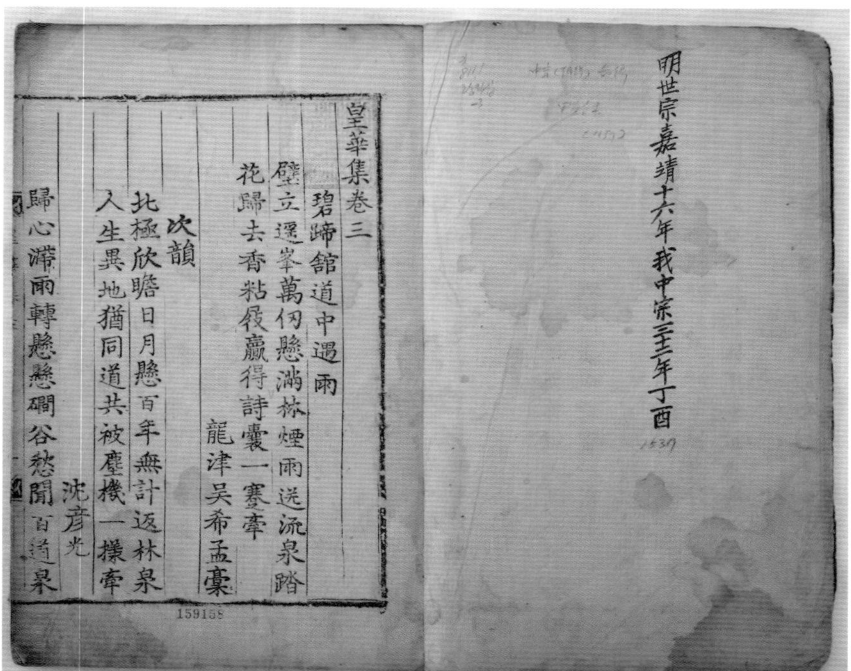

Hwanghwa chip

A collection of poems exchanged between Ming envoys and Chosŏn host officials.

Keimyung University Dongsan Library collection

Plaque at Haeun-jŏng
Written by Chief Ming envoy Gong Yongqing, "Mirror Lake Fishing Village" (鏡湖漁村)

Plaque at Haeun-jŏng
Written by assistant Ming envoy Wu Ximeng, "Small Ocean Cloud Pavilion" (海雲小亭)

Acknowledgements

During the last two years, translating *Travel Log of the Celestial Envoys* has taken me through not only the log itself, but also through the poetry and prose of other members of the Ming embassy of 1537, the *Veritable Records* of the Chosŏn court, gazetteers and geographies, the miscellaneous writings of Chosŏn literati, the Confucian classics and their commentaries, and an array of secondary and tertiary literatures published over three centuries. These are the pleasures, and perhaps indulgences, of the translator of texts produced in "climates of opinion,"[1] to follow Carl Becker, that are now so wholly alien to the present. It is for the most part a solitary labor but despite the passage of weeks and months alone with these texts, I could not have completed this project without the encouragement, help, and patience of others.

I am grateful to Lee Jonghan of Keimyung University, for suggesting that I take on the project in the first place, for his gentle support, and for improving the translation through his careful editing. This translation has also benefited greatly from the modern Korean translation by Kim Yunjo, Yi Chian, and Hwang Tonggwŏn. Their biographical annotations were especially helpful to my understanding of the source text. Kim Paekch'ŏl, my colleague in the Keimyung University Department of History was patient with my awkward Korean and always helpful, both in questions of translation and interpretation and as a lunch partner. Ch'oe Kyŏnghun of the Keimyung University Dongsan Library rare book collection provided me with access to the original manuscript, provided support for my special lecture on the translation project, and has been instrumental in ensuring that the manuscript wends its way through the proper channels of the Keimyung University Press. Nam Kyesun and Kim Chŏnghyŏn, instructors at the Daegu Confucian Academy (大邱鄕校), have been valuable resources whose depth of knowledge and experience I cannot even begin to approach. I am also thankful to Warren Parsons and Jinju Kim who pried me away from my desk for dinner and conversation. Meeting with the members of our reading group, Christian Spahn, Stanley MacLean, Roman Lach, and Lisa Lin, kept me calm and level, even in midweek. Conversations with Jimin Lee and Jake Levine on the nature of translation have expanded my understanding of what it means to engage and translate a text and left me with questions that continue to motivate. And for his rebuilding of body and mind, I am forever grateful to Im Chaeyang.

Finally, there is no way to sufficiently thank Yun Kilsŏp for her intellectual, emotional, and culinary support through the translation of this text. I learned a great deal through our repeated discussion of the *ilgi* and look forward to more in the years to come.

Translation Notes

1 *Travel Log of the Celestial Envoys* is an English translation of *Ch'ŏnsa illo ilgi* 天使一路日記, a manuscript held in the rare book collection of the Keimyung University Dongsan Library. I have undertaken this translation in consultation with the modern Korean translation by Kim Yunjo, Yi Chian, and Hwang Tonggwŏn entitled, *Ch'ŏnsa illo ilgi: Chosŏn, myŏng nara sasin ŭl matta* and published by the Kyemyŏng Taehakkyo Ch'ulp'anbu in 2020. While my English translation is mostly in agreement with the Korean translation by Kim, Yi and Hwang, there are occasional differences arising from different choices in the parsing of the source text, which is unpunctuated. These departures are rare and do not substantially change the text. I have also chosen to maintain the tributary discourse of the source text in the English translation. Hence, I have translated terms like *ch'ŏnsa* 天使 as "celestial envoy" and not "Ming envoy." As I argue in the translator's introduction, this discourse is essential to understanding the political and diplomatic functioning of the text.

2 Time

At the time of this journal, the day was divided into twelve periods, each lasting for approximately two hours. Although I have noted the time of the day on the hour, such as "seven o'clock," the events that are recorded to have happened at a particular time should be understood to have happened in the two-hour period following that hour. Thus, something noted as having happened at seven o'clock happened sometime during the approximately two-hour period starting at seven o'clock, not seven o'clock exactly.

I have converted dates in the translation to the solar calendar with lunar calendar dates in parentheses. Thus, "April 13, 1537 (3/4)" commences with the solar date followed by the lunar date in parentheses in the month/day format; "3/4" indicates the fourth day of the third month of the lunar calendar. All date conversions adhere to the calendrical tables in *Liang qian nian zhong xi li dui zhao biao* 兩千年中西曆對照表 by Xue Zhongsan 薛仲三 and Ouyang Yi 歐陽頤.

3 Place Names

I have not translated most place names, with occasional exceptions for geographical terms such as "river" or "mountain." Most of the stops on the envoys' itinerary are official buildings or office complexes. The terms for these buildings remain untranslated in the main text. The most common of these terms are as follows:

Kwan/gwan 館. This term can refer to a hall in a complex of government offices or to an official guesthouse.

Wŏn 院: This usually refers to an official guesthouse.
Yŏk 驛: This is usually a Chosŏn post station.
Chŏng/jŏng 亭: This is normally, but not always, a single-story pavilion.
Ru/lu/nu 樓: This a raised pavilion of at least two stories with an open upper deck.
Zhan 站: This is usually Ming post station.

4 Official Titles
The translation of official titles follows *The Literati Purges* by Edward Wagner, *Confucian Statecraft and Korean Institutions* by James Palais, *A Dictionary of Official Titles in Imperial China* by Charles Hucker, and *Boundless Winds of Empire* by Sixiang Wang. In cases where a title in the source text did not appear in any of these sources, I have produced an original translation, in consultation with *Kwallyo kigu mit kwanjingmyŏng p'yŏtlam* by O Hŭibok, the *Chŭngbo munhŏn pigo*, compiled by Pak Yongdal *et alia*, and the *Han'guk hanchaŏ sajŏn* compiled by the *Tan'guk Taehakkyo Tongyanghak Yŏn'guso.*

5 Romanization.
I have romanized Korean in McCune-Reischauer and Chinese in Pinyin.

6 Brackets, Parentheses, and Braces
Text in square brackets [...] does not appear in the source text. Text in parentheses (...) appears in the source text but is not necessary for the translation. Text in braces {...} is annotations that appear in the source text.

7 *Chosŏn wangjo sillok* 朝鮮王朝實錄 Citations
Citations of the *Yŏnsan-gun ilgi* 燕山君日記 and the *Chungjong sillok* 中宗實錄 from the *Chosŏn wangjo sillok* are dated as follows: Chosŏn reign year/lunar month/lunar day. For example, *Chungjong sillok* 32/1/2 indicates an entry found for the second lunar day of the first lunar month of the thirty-second year of the reign of King Chungjong.

Table of Contents

Travel Log of the Celestial Envoys (Ch'ŏnsa illo ilgi)

March 30, 1537

(16th year of the Jiajing 嘉靖 Reign, 2nd month, 20th day)

Rain.

At one o'clock in the afternoon (*misi* 未時), the celestial envoys (*ch'ŏnsa* 天使) arrived at the official guesthouse on north bank of the Amnok River (K. Amnok-kang, C. Yalu-jiang 鴨綠江)[01] and commanded the Liaodong 遼東 interpreter Gao Song 高嵩 to shout [across the river to the Chosŏn side], "Interpreter Yi Hwajong 李和宗, gather your paper and brush and come across the river immediately!" The reception envoy (*wŏnjŏpsa* 遠接使) heard this and commanded the interpretation instructor (*yŏkhak hundo* 譯學訓導) Ton

01 While the Chinese reading "Yalu" is more common in English translation, I use the Korean reading "Amnok" as this is a Chosŏn source text.

Paekhyŏng 頓伯衡 to go across forthwith. Soon thereafter the celestial envoys crossed the river and arrived at the official guesthouse on this side of the frontier, whereupon they asked Ton Paekhyŏng, "Why has Yi Hwajong not come and where will the reception envoy meet us?"

Ton Paekhyŏng replied, "The reception envoy and the interpreters, in accordance with precedent, will welcome the imperial proclamation at Ŭisun-gwan 義順館 and so they dare not come." Chang Ŏllyang 張彦良, the magistrate (*moksa* 牧使) of Ŭiju 義州, entered and bowed twice while the envoys sat in chairs and did not return the courtesy. [They] then had tea and commanded Ŏllyang to approach and offer them three cups of wine[02] and then stop.

At three o'clock in the afternoon (*sinsi* 申時), [the envoys] rode in wool-lined palanquins (*chŏn'gyo* 氈轎) to the five-*li* point (*ori-jŏng* 五里程).[03] Magistrate Chang and his assistants donned court attire and prostrated themselves in welcome of the imperial proclamation. Members of the lead group of the entourage, which consisted of the reception envoy, the hospitality envoy (*yŏngwisa* 迎慰使), recorders, interpreters, and physicians, prostrated themselves

---

02 This is *chu* 酒, a general term for alcohol.

03 This term is more commonly rendered as *Ori-jŏng* 五里亭, the "five-*li* pavilion," a pavilion five li outside local government offices where officials welcomed and sent off guest dignitaries. One *li* is approximately one-quarter mile.

in welcome outside the front gate. The envoys entered through the central gate and stepped down from their palanquins at the bottom of the steps where they followed the imperial proclamation into the hall, personally offered it, and then placed it on the desk. They then stood on either side of the imperial tablet (*kwŏlp'ae* 闕牌),[04] facing one another. The reception envoy, the hospitality envoy, recorders, interpreters, and physicians entered the eastern courtyard while all the other staff entered the western courtyard where they performed four bows, offered incense, and performed four more bows. When the ceremony was done, [staff] received the imperial proclamation, took it outside, and enshrined it in the tent [installed for this purpose] behind the main hall. The envoys arrived at the tent and after inspecting the enshrinement of the imperial proclamation, they together went to the eastern chambers (*tonghŏn* 東軒)[05] and then from the eastern chambers to the western chambers. The assistant envoy bid farewell to the chief envoy at the main hall. They saluted one another with a half-bow, hands clasped, and then went up to the eastern and western chambers.

After some time, the envoys donned their formal caps and belts, and went out and sat in the main hall. The special interpreters (*pyŏlt'ongsa* 別通事)

---

04 This tablet represents the person of the Ming emperor.
05 This is a generic term for the main office space of a local or regional government complex.

entered first and performed two bows. The envoys remained seated and clasped their hands, reciprocating the courtesy. The special interpreters then divided and stood on the east and west [walls of the room]. The reception envoy entered and bowed twice to each [envoy]. Then the hospitality envoy entered and bowed twice. The envoys stood and, clasping their hands, performed half bows in reciprocation. Then the recorders, physicians, the various staff, and the protocol inquiry officer (*mullyegwan* 問禮官), one after the other, all performed two bows. Both envoys remained seated and clasped their hands together to reciprocate the courtesy. The protocol inquiry officer submitted the ceremonial notes (*ŭiju* 儀註) and then left.

The envoys then returned to the eastern chambers. Wearing casual clothing, they perused the mounted plaques presented by previous envoys. The command [had gone out to] the local people to prepare in advance a table before the main hall. The interpreter announced the welcoming banquet to the envoys who then again donned their formal caps and belts and sat at the northern wall of the main hall. The reception envoy and the hospitality envoy went before the envoys and saluted. The envoys stood and reciprocated. The reception envoy and the hospitality envoy went and stood along the western wall but the envoys waved to them, asking that they sit down.

The reception envoy and the hospitality envoy sat in chairs and once the tea was complete they produced the list of gifts [presented to the envoys by the Chosŏn king.] Once the envoys had examined the list they said, "It would not be at all appropriate for us to accept these gifts but we do recognize that they amply show the sincere intent of [your] worthy king," and so on. Next [the staff] provided flowers, plates of beef and lamb, aprons, soup, and fruit plates.

The hospitality envoy went to the keg station and poured out some welcome wine (*sŏnwiju* 宣慰酒). He then went before the envoys and saluted (*ŭp* 揖). The chief envoy reciprocated and then took the cup [of welcome wine] and saluted. He then raised the cup and performed a half salute (*panŭp* 半揖) to the assistant envoy. Then he raised his hands and performed a half salute to the reception envoy. He turned back to the hospitality envoy and saluted. The hospitality envoy reciprocated. The chief envoy did not allow the hospitality envoy to take the tray [but rather] drank [the cup of welcome wine] and then gave the empty cup to the hospitality envoy. The hospitality envoy received the empty cup and gave it to an attendant. The hospitality envoy and the chief envoy saluted one another and then the hospitality envoy presented a fruit plate. The chief envoy ate [the fruit] and then clasped his hands [in acknowledgment] to the hospitality envoy.

The hospitality envoy did the same and then instructed the keg station to pour more wine. [With wine in hand], he approached the chief envoy and saluted. The chief envoy reciprocated. The chief envoy then took the cup and saluted the hospitality envoy and the hospitality envoy reciprocated. Once the chief envoy drank [the wine], the hospitality envoy presented a fruit plate. And then he again went to the keg station to pour wine which he took to the assistant envoy and served him in the same fashion as he did the chief envoy above. Then each person took their respective seats and [the servants] brought the soup. The hospitality envoy went to the keg station and poured more wine and then saluted the chief envoy. The envoy reciprocated and then took the cup and saluted the hospitality envoy, raised the cup and did a half salute to the assistant envoy, and a half salute to the reception envoy, and then drank the cup of wine, whereupon he gave back the empty cup as before. [The servants] again served a fruit plate. The chief envoy instructed a servant to go pour more wine and bring it back. [With cup in hand,] he saluted the hospitality envoy who saluted and took the cup. The chief envoy reciprocated the salute. [The hospitality envoy] saluted the assistant envoy who then reciprocated. He then turned back to the chief envoy and saluted and the chief envoy reciprocated. Once the hospitality envoy drank [the cup of wine], he went to the keg station, poured more wine, and served the assistant envoy just as he had the chief envoy. Then he again went to the keg station and poured more wine. He went before the chief envoy and saluted and then offered the final cup. The chief envoy reciprocated the salute, took the cup, and again saluted the hospitality envoy, who reciprocated. Once the chief envoy drank [the cup of wine], he gave the empty cup to the hospitality envoy. The hospitality envoy accepted the empty cup and gave it to a servant. Then he saluted the chief envoy and presented a fruit plate. And then he also presented the final cup [of wine] to the assistant envoy just as he had to the chief envoy. And then the reception envoy served wine [to the envoys] just as the hospitality envoy had. And then [the servants] brought plates of chicken and pork. The hospitality envoy and reception envoy then served the envoys wine again just as they had done before. The envoys said, "The night is growing late and, moreover, we are drunk. You may stop the wine."[06] And so ended the banquet.

The hospitality envoy inquired as to their comfort and the chief envoy said, "Today's ample ceremonies have shown the sincere intent of [your]

06 While source text indicates that both envoys (*yangsa* 兩使) are speaking, it is most likely that it was chief envoy who spoke. This is likely the case in each instance in which direct quotations are attributed to both envoys simultaneously.

king. We and our entourage are in no position to be able to consume the entirety of the table that you have prepared for us. You may have the local officials take what remains." They moved their chairs and sat in the middle [of the chamber] and said, "You may remove [the leftover food] now while we are still here."

The reception envoy instructed the interpreter to say, "Are we to give the food left over from the banquet to the servants?"

The envoys replied, "The entirety of our entourage has partaken in the banquet so you may distribute whatever food remains, but you may not give out uncooked food or pastries."

The envoys spoke quietly with one another and then asked the interpreter, "In what year did Capital Magistrate (*p'anyun* 判尹) O 吳[07] pass the civil service examination?"

The interpreter replied, "He passed in 1504."

"And what in year did Minister (*p'ansŏ* 判書) Chŏng 鄭 pass?"[08]

The interpreter replied, "He passed in 1509." They also asked whether the ranks of Capital Magistrate O and Minister Chŏng were high or low.

---

07 "Capital Magistrate O" refers to O Kyŏl 吳潔

08 This is the reception envoy Chŏng Saryong 鄭士龍. The envoys often refer to him simply as "minister" (C. *panshu*, K. *p'ansŏ* 判書).

The interpreter replied, "They are both senior second rank."

P'yŏngan 平安 Provincial Inspector (*tosa* 都事) An Su 安琇 offered his salutations. The chief envoy said, "What kind of official is a provincial inspector?"

The interpreter replied, "The provincial inspector is a secretary (*nanggwan* 郎官) in the office of the governor of this province. It is a civil appointment (*munjik* 文職)."

During the banquet the envoys said, "This country always maintains ritual propriety; we are already so weary of hearing about it so we did not bother to ask about any of the ritual texts throughout the whole process."

When the chief envoy saw the rice porridge he asked, "Is this hot or cold."

The interpreter replied, "This is cold porridge but there is also hot porridge."

The chief envoy said, "Have this boiled again." So it was done and the envoys nearly finished a whole bowl full.

The envoys then retired to their quarters. The hospitality envoy had the interpreter deliver the list of gift clothing [from the king] to each envoy. The chief envoy examined the list and laughed, "I am not now meeting with the king so why should I receive gifts?[09] Moreover, such a list should be written on red paper and sealed in a red envelope. That would have been appropriate. The capital magistrate is surely a man who knows ceremonial protocol. How could he have used white paper?"

Yi Hwajong replied, "The use of red paper for gift lists has never been a custom of this country."

The envoys said, "Tomorrow we will reconsider and discuss it."

When the envoys crossed the river on this day, they sent back nineteen musicians [to Ming]. When [the envoys] reached Ŭisun-gwan in Ŭiju, they used a vermillion brush to cross out the names [of the musicians] from the manifest. The envoys called an interpreter and said, "Where will we spend the night tomorrow?"

The interpreter replied, "We will spend the night at Yangch'aek-kwan 良策館."

The envoys said, "Draft a document indicating the distances and names of all the places where we will stop between here and the capital." The reception envoy had [an officer] write down all the station stops and the distances between them as well the surnames, given names, and titles of the entire

---

09 Gong Yongqing 龔用卿, the chief envoy, here makes the point that he will not receive gifts from the king unless the king gives them personally.

entourage and all the staff along the way and the presented it to the envoys.

The chief envoy said to Yi Hwajong, "[Our] court loves your country deeply and so especially sent word of the felicitous event."[10]

Yi Hwajong said, "[Your] court has given solace and aid to our country; all the officials and the people gratefully accept the imperial grace," and then asked about Annam, namely whether or not [the Ming court] had also informed [the Annam court].

The chief envoy said, "Not yet. [The imperial proclamation] has gone only to the thirteen [Ming] provincial governors, Nanjing 南京, and this country. [No others have yet received it]."

Yi Hwajong also asked, "In addition to the imperial proclamation, there are also two edicts. What are they?"

The chief envoy replied, "The edicts are not related to your country, only to our embassy."

Hwajong also asked, "Are there now any [imperial] gifts to bestow?"

The chief envoy replied, "The bestowal of [imperial] gifts is a matter to be discussed in meetings with high officials at a later date."

The hospitality envoy took the clothing and other items that had come

10 This is a reference to the birth of the imperial crown prince.

from the capital and distributed them to the attendants (*tumok* 頭目)[11] in the envoys' entourage but they all refused to accept, saying, "You should request that Grandfather (*laodie* 老爹)[12] take care of this; it is not appropriate for us to accept it now." In the evening, there was a banquet for the attendants just outside the central gate. {This was entirely the same as the banquet for the envoys. There was precedent for an attendants' banquet already but from here after attendants' banquets followed this [example].}[13]

March 31, 1537

(2/21)

Rain.

The hospitality envoy again brought up the issue of the clothing [the

11 The term *tumok*, translated here as "attendant," refers merchants who traveled with the envoys to do business in Chosŏn. There were many of these men on any given mission and they performed a number of semi-official duties as runners and assistants to the envoys. On this particular mission, their commercial transactions in Seoul, in which both the Ming envoys and a number of Chosŏn officials appear to have been involved, came to the attention of King Chungjong on multiple occasions. See *Chungjong sillok* 32/3/11-16.

12 In this context this, is a term of both respect and affection. In this instance, it refers to the chief envoy.

13 This is an annotation in the original text.

king sent] and the assistant envoy said, "Although these gifts are borne of generous intent, we must not accept them."

The hospitality envoy again pleaded, "These are clothes His Majesty has sent to [your] attendants. We beg you to permit us to distribute them."

The assistant envoy replied, "When we meet and bow before His Majesty, then we will consider how to deal with this." Protocol Inquiry Officer Im P'irhyŏng 任弼亨 again asked if the ceremonial notes were acceptable. The envoys replied, "We should talk about this once we arrive at Sinan-gwan 新安館. Go there in advance and wait."

The chief envoy then went to the assistant envoy's quarters, saying, "It is raining today. Even though we are unable to depart, it will not be necessary to meet with the minister."

At nine o'clock in the morning (*sasi* 巳時), the envoys sat together in the eastern chambers, ate breakfast, and then quickly summoned Yi Hwajong, saying, "We must leave immediately." When he [went to] speak to the minister, the rain was steady and the road was quite muddy. The reception envoy went to the quarters of the chief envoy with the intention of delaying [the departure]. The chief envoy quickly emerged and sat in the main hall. The assistant envoy did the same.

The reception envoy then went before them, saluted, and then said,

"Now the hour is already late but the rain has not stopped. The road ahead is long and I am afraid that the palanquin bearers may slip and fall. This is my concern."

The chief envoy said, "The minister's request that we stay is [merely] a courtesy of the host, but we are on an errand of the sovereign and must not tarry. The minister has amply shown His Majesty's intent to honor us, his guests. This we already know so we have decided that we must not tarry any longer. In the present situation, spring weather is frequently rainy, and it is difficult to know in advance whether tomorrow there will be rain or shine." The envoys quickly called for oil paper with which they first wrapped the imperial proclamation and edicts, then the tokens of their offices[14] and other such items, and then, finally, they went out into the rain. [The procession] traveled ten *li* before the rain stopped. The envoys then got out of the wool-insulated palanquins and continued riding in regular palanquins (*p'yŏnggyo* 平轎). They arrived at Sogok-kwan 所串館 and had lunch.

As soon as the procession arrived at Yangch'aek-kwan in the early evening, the banquet began. The envoys came out and had tea. Once that

14 The tokens of office are the commission (*chŏl* 節) and the ax (*wŏl* 鉞). The commission is the documentation of the authority granted an officer by the sovereign. The ax is a symbol of the authority of an officer to execute those under his command, should he deem such punishment necessary.

was complete, they had dinner with the reception envoy, drank one round of wine, and then stopped. The envoys hosted the minister, conducting the protocols with the utmost respect. In the morning on this day, when the procession was still at Ŭisun-gwan, one of the staff failed to maintain his post and so [an officer] beat his buttocks with a staff. That evening, three others were also beaten who failed to carry out their duties.

April 1, 1537

(2/22)

High winds and rain.

The envoys emerged and sat in the main hall where they ate breakfast together. The reception envoy wished to enter and conduct the routine ceremonies but the envoys stopped him, saying, "We have just sat down in our casual clothing; we cannot meet with a person in cap and belt." After they had eaten, they changed their clothes and came out and stood [in the main hall] as the reception envoy came in to meet them.

They instructed him to report and he said, "Today, the road ahead is still long and also rainy and wet. We cannot light our torches and thus we will surely lose our way. Moreover, the people of this country are not accustomed to shouldering such loads. If they travel on the slippery road, we are not without the concern that they will slip in the mud and drop [the palanquins they] bear. We ask that we stay here for a little while and then reconsider conditions tomorrow." The envoys permitted this. Indeed, they seemed quite happy about it.

The reception envoy then asked, "Our small country reveres and places great importance on imperial proclamations and edicts. Precedent calls for the selection of an auspicious day (*kiril* 吉日) for the announcement [of the content of the document]. Thus I have dared to report."

The envoys said, "This is proper and good. We should follow the practice of this country. If it is too far into the future, however, we will not be able to stay for it, and if it is too soon, we fear the rain may delay us and we will not be able to reach [the capital in time]. Divine a tentative day and then report back [for our approval]."

The reception envoy replied, "The difference between the sooner and later dates will not be any more than a day or two." He also asked about the content of the two imperial edicts [the envoys had received] and whether or not there were any gifts [from the emperor].

The chief envoy replied, "Only the imperial proclamation is for this country. As for the two edicts, one concerns the security [protocols] of our mission and the other is the imperial warrant authorizing the mission. The [Ming] court has broadly spread the news of this felicitous event through the empire and in recognition of the fact that your country has diligently and humbly submitted tribute with unmatched sincerity, the court has especially commanded this report [of the birth of the prince]. This is no different than [the proclamation] to the [Ming] interior nobles (*nei zhuhou* 內諸侯), with the sole exception that there are no gifts."

In the afternoon, the extended-stay banquet (*yuil yŏn* 留日宴) began and the envoys came out, sat down, and dined together with the reception envoy. They joined clasped their hands together in salutation and said, "Today we have accepted the request to delay our departure and indeed the courtesy [of this banquet] has been exceptional. Many thanks, many thanks!"

As they were drinking wine, the envoys saw the sliced octopus on the table and indicated they wanted to see a whole one, saying, "We want to see a live one!"

Usually when serving wine, precedent requires that once the celestial envoys have drunk, the host must raise his hands and offer a fruit plate, but this time the host did not do so. The envoys had [a servant] offer the fruit plate to the reception envoy, but he refused and did not dare to accept. The envoys said, "This is what we want, please do not refuse!"

The chief envoy called to the attendant Cui Zhong 崔忠 and asked him, "When Compiler (*taishi* 太史) Tang 唐 came here, you accompanied him.[15] Did he receive the ministers of this country in the same way I have? This is an important official of this country and I am only concerned that I may have made a mistake."

Cui Zhong said, "Compiler Tang received the high officials exactly as you have, Grandfather."

The banquet ended and the envoys summoned Yi Hwajong, "We are so very pleased that the minister is a man of such refinement!"

When the banquet started today, the envoys held single flowers and looked at them in great detail, not affixing them [to their clothing] for quite some time. It seemed as if they were wondering if they had been offered the same flowers over and over again.

---

15 Tang Gao 唐皐 (1469-1526) was the Ming envoy who arrived in Chosŏn in 1521 to announce the enthronement of the Ming Jiajing Emperor.

April 2, 1537

(2/23)

Clear.

At seven o'clock in the morning (*chinsi* 辰時), the envoys and the reception envoy met in the main hall and ate breakfast together. They departed and later arrived at Tongnim Fortress (Tongnim-sŏng 東林城). The chief envoy summoned Yi Hwajong and asked him, "What is the name of this fortress?"

Yi replied, "This is the old Tongnim Fortress. It dates to an age long ago; we cannot know exactly." The chief envoy accidentally dropped a book from the palanquin. It turned out to be a hand-copied edition of *Brilliant Flowers Anthology* (*Hwanghwa chip* 皇華集).[16] The protocol inquiry officer presented the ceremonial notes and [the chief envoy] perused them in the palanquin.

At eleven o'clock in the morning (*osi* 午時), they arrived at Kŏryŏn-gwan

16 This is an anthology of poetry written by Ming envoys and their Chosŏn hosts. The anthology is amended to include the new poems that each successive mission produces. See Sixiang Wang, *Boundless Winds of Empire*, chapter 8. Here I follow Wang's translation of the title.

車輦館. The envoys descended from their palanquins and went directly under the "coiled pine" (*pansong* 盤松) and clapped their hands together, declaring, "So this is the fabled 'coiled pine'!" Then they went into the offices and sat in the main hall. They asked Yi Hwajong, "Where are the Tomb of Kija (Kija-myo 箕子墓), P'ungwŏl-lu 風月樓, and Ch'ongsu Mountain (Ch'ongsu-san 葱秀山)?"

Yi replied, "The Tomb of Kija and P'ungwŏl Pavilion are in P'yŏngyang 平壤, six days journey from here. Ch'ongsu Mountain is in P'yŏngsan 平山, Hwanghae Province (Hwanghae-do 黃海道).

The chief envoy then asked, "Are there hereditary bureaucratic appointments in this country?"

Hwajong replied, "Those who have attained military merit [may] receive hereditary bureaucratic appointments but for civil officials, even in cases outstanding talent, there is no such practice."

The chief envoy said, "If that is the case, are the sons of high officials unable to secure official positions?"

Yi replied, "If they are men of talent who can be employed, then the Ministry of Personnel or the Ministry of War will employ them."

[The envoys] departed after lunch. While they were on the road, the chief envoy summoned Yi Hwajong and asked, "With which lands is your country adjacent in the north, south, east, and west?"

Yi replied, "To the north is Jianzhou 建州, to the southeast is the sea, and to the west is the Amnok River."

The chief envoy said, "What land does the southeastern sea reach?"

"Japan," Yi replied.

The chief envoy said, "Are there any people who travel back and forth [between Chosŏn and Japan]?"

Yi replied, "In years past, Japanese merchants (*sangwae* 商倭)[17] sometimes came and bought and sold goods on the frontier, but later they behaved improperly so we ceased interactions with them."

The chief envoy asked, "Do people from Liuqiu 琉球 come to this land?"

Yi replied, "No."

At three o'clock in the afternoon, the embassy arrived at Imban-gwan 林畔館. There were onlookers in front of the offices, gathering in groups and encroaching upon the road. The disciplinary officer (*kohwŏn'gwan* 考喧官) had one of the station slaves (*chorye* 皂隸) grab one by the hair and shout at him to stop. The chief envoy summoned Yi Hwajong and asked, "Why did

17 "Wae" 倭 here refers to the Japanese.

the station slave beat that man?"

Yi replied, "This mob of idlers was encroaching upon the road and it seemed like it was going flood across it in disrespect. We [sought] only to stop it."

The chief envoy said, "They are causing no harm. Tell the minister immediately not to stop them again – let them look on as they please."

The reception envoy had Yi Hwajong ask the chief envoy, "Has the [imperial] court already invested the prince as the heir apparent?"

He replied, "You have asked about this, but at this moment the investiture has not taken place. When we reached Liaodong, we heard that all the civil and military officials had requested the investiture, but the emperor maintained that it was still too early and refused to heed their pleas. It thus appears that if the investiture will not occur this year, [the court] will decide upon the investiture next year. Another proclamation envoy (*zhaoshi* 詔使) will certainly come [to Chosŏn]."

At five o'clock in the evening (*yusi* 酉時), the banquet began and everyone drank wine. When the assistant envoy left to relieve himself, the chief envoy asked Yi Hwajong, "The king [of Chosŏn] has been on the throne for, I think, fourteen or fifteen years now?"

Yi replied, "It has already been thirty years."

The chief envoy said, "When Compiler Tang came, was it not 1521?"

Yi replied, "Envoy Tang came to deliver the proclamation of the enthronement [of the Jiajing Emperor]. The king [of Chosŏn] had already ascended the throne in 1506. At that time the chief eunuch had come to deliver an imperial message [to the king of Chosŏn]."

The chief envoy said, "How could the chief eunuch come to deliver the imperial message?" He also asked, "How many in the [Chosŏn] royal capital can speak Chinese?"

Yi replied, "There are many."

The chief envoy said, "Next year the proclamation envoy will be able to hold conversations [on his own]." He also asked, "Why is only Scholar Sŏ (Sŏ haksa 徐學士)[18] absent from the *Brilliant Flowers Anthology*?"

Yi replied, "At that time, they did not compose many poems so there was no new compilation. There were only a few poems hung on the wall at Unhŭng-gwan 雲興館."

The chief envoy also asked, "What was the name of the [Chosŏn] minister who came [to Ming] as the Congratulatory and Winter Solstice Envoy (*jinhe dongzhi zaixiang* 進賀冬至宰相)?"

18 This is a reference to Sŏ Kŏjŏng 徐居正, the reception envoy for the Ming envoys Qi Shun 祈順 and Zhang Jin 張瑾 in 1476.

Yi replied, "Cho In'gyu 趙仁奎."

The chief envoy said, "Last winter, Master Shi Daɔ 史道[19] and I attended [the imperial] court together." They had another round of wine and then the envoys wanted to end the banquet. The reception envoy then got up and stood next to the table and asked to serve them one more cup. They permitted this.

The banquet ended and the envoys stood up from the table and asked the interpreter, "Why did the minister not leave through the front courtyard?"

The interpreter replied, "Both of you, Grandfathers, were still seated and he cautiously went behind the building when he left."

The envoys said, "That can be said to be in accordance with propriety." They also asked Yi Hwajong, "Does the minister know that we are quite pleased?"

Yi replied, "How could he not know? His only concern is that there may have been some protocol inadvertently omitted – a concern that grows more serious by the day."

The envoys said, "The minister is a man of substance and, moreover, he

---

19 Shi Dao was the assistant envoy who, along with the chief envoy Tang Gao, came to Chosŏn in 1521 to announce the enthronement of the Ming Jiajing Emperor.

knows ritual propriety. We are both very pleased. You must tell him this."

They also had Yi Hwajong say to the reception envoy, "Write down the name of each and every ancient ruin, mountain, and river along the route from Ŭiju down to the royal capital and also enumerate the titles and ranks of every official assigned to each government office in the royal capital and then return [these lists to us]." [The Chosŏn staff] wrote up the lists generally as they had been instructed and delivered them [to the envoys]. The assistant envoy bound them into a book of about 15 or 16 sections, wrote a formal cover letter, and then had the staff at Imban-gwan send it back to Tang-zhan 湯站.[20]

April 3, 1537

(2/24)

Clear.

The envoys sat together in the main hall and once they finished their

20 Tang-zhan was a Ming post station just north of the Yalu River.

meal they summoned the reception envoy. They saluted [one another] and then [the envoys] departed. They went not even seven or eight *li* before mounting horses and riding another ten *li* and arriving at the north bank of the Tongno River (Tongno-ha 同爐河). Seeing the rocky crag at the side of the road, the envoys both dismounted and climbed to the top to survey the view. Afterwards they returned to their palanquins and reached Unhŭng-gwan 雲興館 where they summoned the reception envoy to dine with them. Through the interpreter Yi Hwajong, they said, "We are very happy with the minister's attitude and etiquette. Only our languages are different; what a shame! Master Shi said to us, 'The attitudes and etiquette of the Chosŏn lord and his ministers are something to see!' and now we know that this is true." [Later] in passing a memorial gate for a filial daughter (*hyonyŏ chŏngmun* 孝女旌門), the envoys descended from their palanquins and rubbed their hands over the stele as they read its inscription.

At three o'clock in the afternoon, they arrived at Chŏngju 定州. The chief magistrate (*suryŏng* 守令) and his office staff came to meet the imperial proclamation at the five-*li* point and then [accompanied it] to the magistracy officers. The special hospitality envoy (*pyŏryŏngwisa* 別迎慰使), Third Royal Secretary (*usŭngji* 右承旨) Kim Mi 金亹, instructed the magistrate and his staff to separate themselves into eastern and western files. {The reception envoy stood in the eastern file while the magistrate and his staff stood in the western file. This protocol remained the same hereafter.}[21] After receiving the imperial proclamation, the envoys each went to their quarters. Before long they came out and sat in the main hall. The reception envoy and the hospitality envoy came in and greeted them. The protocol inquiry officer then presented the ceremonial notes. The envoys said, "What is the distance between the [capital] city gate and the royal palace? What is the distance between the place where [the king] will welcome the imperial proclamation and the city gate?"

The protocol inquiry officer replied, "It is about eight or nine *li* from the royal palace to the city gate and about four or five *li* from the city gate to the outer city environs.

The chief envoy said, "Why have you presented the ceremonial notes without recording [these distances]? There are occasional errors in the ceremonial notes for the tea as well, but these are not serious and you need not worry about them. However, the five bows and three prostrations (*wu bai san koutou* 五拜三叩頭) are universal protocols practiced throughout the world. Why is this item now absent from the ceremonial notes?"

21 This is annotation in the original manuscript.

The protocol inquiry officer [and the envoys] debated back and forth and then the envoys said, "Every time envoys have come [to Chosŏn] to deliver an imperial proclamation there have been errors in protocol, but [Chosŏn] must not adopt them as precedents. You refer to the "Protocols of the *Hongwu* Era" (*Hongwu lizhi* 洪武禮制) [to justify your position], but at that time [in the *Hongwu* Era],[22] how could there have been an established protocol for informing a foreign state (*waiguo* 外國) of the felicitous event of the birth of an imperial crown prince? When we passed Guangning 廣寧 on our way here, the report had been made to the Nine Imperial Ancestral Shrines and the blanket amnesty arrived. The [officials of the] three offices [of the Guangning government] came out from the city and performed the five bows and three prostrations. How could it be possible to take this protocol implemented throughout the Central State (*Zhongguo* 中國) and not implement it in the Eastern State (*Dongguo* 東國)?[23] You must return immediately [to Seoul], report to His Highness, correct the ceremonial notes, and then return."

As the sun began to set, the welcoming banquet began. Once the

22 This is the reign period of the first Ming emperor, Taizu 太祖, r. 1368-1398.

23 The central state here is the Ming Empire and the Eastern State is Chosŏn, located to the east of Ming.

tea was over, the reception envoy and the hospitality envoy instructed Yi Hwajong to tell the envoys, "Customarily, we have conducted offerings at this fortification. Precedent calls for a musical performance. Thus we have dared to report to the envoys."

"What sort of music is this 'musical performance' and does it not include ladies?

"Indeed, it is a female musical performance."

The envoys looked at one another and said, "We have no use for this."

The reception envoy and the hospitality envoy pleaded once more, "His Highness has especially sent his closest subjects to conduct the offering. If there is no music, the rites will be incomplete, and this, we fear, will be most inelegant."

The envoys asked, "Have previous proclamation envoys partaken in this?" And then they stated, "The will of His Highness is thus, but we strongly wish to avoid following it. It would be acceptable to have the first performance, but stop after that." The performance was carried out in accordance with this instruction. Once it was over, the reception envoy and the hospitality envoy both offered two rounds of wine and then stopped.

The chief envoy asked the reception envoy, "You said that your country holds civil service examinations triennially but did [the interpreter] not say that you passed the exam in 1509?"[24]

The reception envoy replied, "It is the custom of this country to select men [for government service] in irregularly scheduled years as well. This is called a 'special examination' (*pyŏlsi* 別試)."

"Why is it called a 'special examination'?"

"When there is an unexpected felicitous occasion, the state selects men [for government service]."

The chief envoy said, "Does [the state] examine and select only scholars from the national academy (*guoxue* 國學)?"[25]

The reception envoy replied, "Any scholar from across the four corners of the country can sit for the examination and be selected."

The chief envoy said, "In the Yongle 永樂 Era,[26] Master He 河[27] sat for this sort of exam. Your country must be following this model."

The envoys were sitting in the eastern chambers and as they were inspecting the roster of attendants, they asked, "Why have Gao Song's

---

24 Here the chief envoy notes that the reception envoy previously told him that the Chosŏn exams were held in years ending in the characters *cha* 子, *o* 午, *myo* 卯, and *yu* 酉, according to the two-character designations of the sexagenary cycle. The host envoy, however passed the exam in 1509, a year ending in the character *sa* 巳.

25 The "national academy" should be understood to refer to the Sŏnggyun-gwan 成均館, the highest institution of learning from whence much of the Chosŏn bureaucracy was appointed.

26 This is the reign period of the third Ming emperor, Taizong 太宗, r. 1403-1424.

27 The identity of Master He is unclear.

family members come along?" It seemed that they wished to report this as a violation, but upon further inspection of his documention, they did not. Gao Song had stolen a beeswax candle from the chambers while three people from his household looked out through gaps in the shutters [to see if anyone was coming], so the chief envoy had each of them beaten four or five times with a staff.

April 4, 1537

(2/25)

Clear.

At seven o'clock in the morning, the envoys departed and later arrived at Napch'ŏng-jŏng 納清亭. After perusing the plaques, the assistant envoy pointed to the three characters on the pavilion title plaque, *nap* 納, *ch'ŏng* 淸, and *chŏng* 亭, and said, "The calligraphy is not good. Grandfather Gong[28] writes large characters quite well; why not ask him to rewrite it?"

28 This is a reference to Gong Yongqing, the chief envoy.

Soon thereafter [the envoys] summoned the reception envoy and they ate lunch together. The reception envoy asked of the envoys, "We do not know how long ago this place fell into obscurity, but fortunately it met with the appreciation of Grandfathers Tang and Shi[29] who have already named the pavilion and written an account [of this place], making these mountains and streams outshine the rest of the region. Now once more we meet with two grandfathers who have come bearing an imperial proclamation. If you were to show us favor and rewrite [the text of] the pavilion title plaque, how could it not cause this place to shine even more brightly? This is what I dare to request of you."

The chief envoy replied, "Neither calligraphy nor poetry are things of which I am capable. It would be best to ask Grandfather Wu[30] to do it."

After lunch the host envoy served two or three rounds of wine and the chief envoy said, "Minister, you have brought members of your household [along on this journey]. Are there any able archers among them?"

"There are."

"I wish to see them shoot before we arrive at Kasan 嘉山."

29 This is a reference to the Ming Chief Envoy Tang Gao 唐皐 and assistant envoy Shi Dao 史道 who were dispatched to Chosŏn in 1521.

30 This is a reference to the assistant envoy Wu Ximeng 吳希盟.

At three o'clock in the afternoon, they reached Kap'yŏng-gwan 嘉平館. The envoys changed into casual clothes and went up to the eastern chambers and then later to the pavilion. They quickly asked the host envoy, "Bring the archers!" The host envoy entered [the pavilion], saluted, and sat down, instructing eighteen archers selected from P'yŏngan Province *(P'yŏngan-do* 平安道) to stand in a line and shoot at a target 170 paces distant: three rounds of ten arrows each. The envoys sat down and watched from the forward columns [of the office]. In the evening they personally compared the high and low scores of the day and then stood up before the banquet table and, in the order of the scores, awarded wine and endless praise to the archers. The envoys already knew the Ŭiju military officer Sŏ Kyŏngch'ŏn 徐慶千, a military officer from Ŭiju, was a member of the host envoy's household. As soon as Sŏ began to shoot, the envoys looked at one another and praised him. When he finished, they said to the minister, "This member of your household shoots exceptionally well. I imagine he has already passed the military exams."

The host envoy replied, "He has indeed passed the military exams as you say, but recently there has been a reorganization of bureaucratic posts so now he will follow me."

Then the envoys said to Cho Sebong 趙世鳳, "Both you and your son shoot very well and are worthy of recognition." Cho Sebong's son is Cho Ŏnp'il 曺彦弼, one of the archers in the demonstration. The host envoy asked the envoys to show him the top scorers from the day's shoot, but they said, "The hour is already late. Wait until later and then we can look at it."

Once the envoys' quarters were prepared for the evening and wine was served, the envoys laughed and said, "Each day we have been learning a few words of the local language of this country. It would be great if you, too, minister, start from today with the phrase, 'Let's have a drink'!" [in Chinese].

The host envoy grabbed a cup, approached the envoys, and said in Chinese, "Let's have a drink!"

The envoys laughed, "You have learned correctly!"

The host envoy then said, "I want to have the entire staff raise their cups in honor of the envoys but out of fear and deference, I simply dare not open my mouth." The envoys allowed it.

When Hong Ch'un'gyŏng 洪春卿 raised his cup, the envoys said, "You are a man of outstanding talent; you will surely receive high appointments quickly." When Pak Ch'ungwŏn 朴忠元 raised his cup, the envoys said, "You are a young man of great talent; your king must be very pleased."

The host envoy again set up a small target under torchlight and had the archers shoot at it. All of them hit the target seven or eight times out of ten. The envoys again came out and watched from the forward pillars. The host envoy then asked of the envoys, "This pavilion has heretofore been remote, old, and unknown, but now you two august gentlemen have stayed here. If you were to give it a name, how could it not be a matter of great fortune to all the mountains and streams of this area?" The envoys assented.

April 5, 1537

(2/26)

Clear.

The envoys emerged from the main hall and sat down. The host envoy saluted them and they all sat together and had breakfast. The chief envoy said, "As for the pavilion name you requested yesterday, Grandfather Wu decided on "Qishan" 齊山.

The assistant envoy said, "It would be good to have Grandfather

Gong's calligraphy."

The chief envoy added, "One of the two of us should write an explanation of the meaning of the name."

[We] again presented the itinerary to Seoul. The envoys examined it and then passed it on to an attendant. The envoys departed and arrived at Chŏkkae-jŏng 敵愾亭 at nine o'clock in the morning. The envoys asked about the name of the pavilion and when they received the answer "Chŏkkae," the chief envoy said, "The name of the pavilion does not match the landscape."[31]

The assistant envoy replied, "It would be fitting, grandfather, if you were to name it."

The envoys called upon the reception envoy and, sitting together with him, said, "Today we want to see some fishing!" The reception envoy immediately had a fisherman launch a little boat and cast his net into the

---

31 The words *chŏk* 敵 and *kae* 愾, literally "enemy" and "rage/anger," are an allusion to a line from the *Zuo Tradition* (*Zuo zhuan* 左傳), part of a passage in which Ning Wuzi of Wei 衛甯武子 explains the appropriate behavior of a "subordinate subject" (*peichen* 陪臣) before Lord Wen 文公. Following the translation of Durrant, Li, and Schaberg, with slight modification, "The princes would take as enemy whomsoever the king raged against and offer their achievements" (諸侯敵王所愾而獻其功). The name of the pavilion is thus a rather bellicose statement of loyalty to the sovereign by taking the enemies of the king to be one's own enemies. See Feng Lihua and Lu Hao, eds., *Jingjiao zuo xiu* (Shanghai: Huiwentang, 1911): 8:7a-b; *Zuo Tradition, Volume One* trans. Stephen Durant, Wai-yee Li, and David Schaburg (Seattle: University of Washington Press, 2016), 484-5.

river. It was just at this moment that the reception envoy had some live carp taken from the kitchen and surreptitiously laid in the bottom of the boat so that it looked as though they had just then been caught in the net. The envoys were delighted and went down the stairs from the pavilion to go take a closer look. The fish were slick and leaping so [a servant] quickly fetched a water jug to put them in. Once the fish were secure, the envoys had half of them sent to the cook.

After lunch the envoys walked [to the river] and boarded an official yacht (*nusŏn* 樓船), calling the reception envoy join them. They sat together and talked and laughed and thoroughly enjoyed themselves. The chief envoy said, "This pavilion is built on the riverside and surrounded by river mists so it should be called "Embracing River" (Gong-jiang 控江). Moreover, it is a metaphor for how the court embraces the king. I should write a plaque text."

The reception envoy thanked him and said, "This remote and rustic landscape has received so many beautiful names, how could this be anything other than deeply auspicious?"

Out in the middle of the river, the reception envoy encouraged them to drink and after eight or nine rounds, a small boat from the far shore netted some fish and approached. The envoys were very pleased and had a wonderful time.

The envoys arrived at the Ch'ŏngchŏn River (Ch'ŏngch'ŏn-gang 淸川江) at one o'clock in the afternoon. They again called for the host envoy and they sat together on the official yacht. Once more, the reception envoy had some local villagers net some fish, as had been done previously on the Pakch'ŏn River (Pakch'ŏn-gang 博川江), and bring them to the envoys, who were again delighted. They drank several rounds before stopping. The envoys saw that local onlookers on the river banks were prevented from watching the entourage and the chief envoy said, "The arrival of a message from the emperor of the Great Ming in the Eastern State is truly a fortunate and felicitous event. Everyone from the highest ministers to the common people should gather to see it. Really, do not shout at them to stop."

The magistrate of Anju 安州 and the various royal commissioners who had come out to the station all gathered at the riverside to welcome the imperial proclamation. They left their boat and later arrived at Anhŭng-gwan. Hospitality envoy Yun Anin 尹安仁, P'yŏngan Provincial Governor Yi Kwiryŏng 李龜齡, and all the various royal commissioners divided themselves into eastern and western files and bowed to the imperial proclamation and then greeted the envoys individually. The entire gathering then departed for Paeksang-nu 百祥樓. [The envoys] gasped in astonishment as they viewed the landscape from the river. The chief envoy said, "There is outstanding landscape like this in my home region and yet, looking at this now, I do not think it compares. An island distant and water sparkling, my home cannot match this! After we have delivered the imperial proclamation and met the king, I should write a text and have it carved upon a plaque and hung [in the pavilion here]. On the way back, we will have to return here to relax and look around before leaving [Chosŏn]." He also commanded the archers to shoot one round of targets.

The chief envoy saw that the assistant Paek Such'ŏn 白壽千 was quite bright and asked him, "Have you read many books?"

"I have read only *The Great Learning*" (*Taehak* 大學)

Both envoys recited the introduction and the main text of *The Great Learning* and then asked Paek, "Why should a literate youth such as yourself be satisfied with this menial labor?"

The translator said, "He was originally only errand boy, but he taught himself to read."

The envoys were astounded, proclaiming, "When even the errand boy can read, I can now believe that in the Eastern Region (Dongfang 東方),[32] every

32 This a reference to Chosŏn, a region to the east of the Ming Empire.

family reads and every household maintains propriety and righteousness!" They then called upon the interpreter and the attending physician to recite Zhu Xi's 朱熹 *Commentary on the Great Learning* (*Daxue zhangju* 大學章句), for which they rewarded them with wine and food.

At nine o'clock in the evening, the envoys returned to Anhŭng-gwan. The attendant to the assistant envoy, Commander Tian Lu 田祿, was late in bringing back a trunk. Chŏng Yunsŏng 鄭允誠, magistrate of Hŭich'ŏn County (Hŭich'ŏn-gun 熙川郡), grabbed him by the coat and yelled at him. The reception envoy heard about it and issued a command to the interpreters, "This is a local official [Chŏng Yunsŏng]. If even the grandfathers[33] themselves did not reprimand the attendant like this, how could Chŏng have possibly been justified in yelling at him so? We must inform the celestial envoys."

Gao Song and other attendants thanked [the host official] and said, "They truly did not understand the situation and behaved thoughtlessly. If you report this to the envoys, you will find that there were many others involved. Please forgive them."

The envoys summoned Yi Hwajong and said, "The scholars of your country by protocol do not come out to welcome the imperial

33 This is a reference to the envoys.

proclamation?"

Hwajong responded, "The national custom is that scholars in both the capital and provinces remain in their academies and read their texts, nothing more. It is not like the Central State where scholars stand in file and participate in state ritual, so we simply do not command them to welcome the imperial proclamation."

The envoys said, "If scholars are not to welcome imperial proclamations, why did the Compiler Tang write a poem for the scholars of Chŏngju?"

Hwajong said, "Envoy Tang arrived in Chŏngju on his way back. He gathered the local scholars to test and observe their character. They did not appear in order to welcome an imperial proclamation."

The envoys said, "Fundamentally, scholars must maintain propriety and righteousness. How can they fail to carry out such an important protocol as welcoming an imperial proclamation? Inform the minister that from now on the scholars must gather to welcome the imperial proclamation."

The reception envoy replied, "Since we have never had this protocol in the past, I should inform His Majesty and make the necessary arrangements." The envoys then commanded that the welcome banquet be postponed until the following day.

April 6, 1537

(2/27)

Rain.

The welcoming banquet in Anju 安州 was prepared in the main hall at the magistracy office. The envoys came out and took their seats. The reception envoy and hospitality envoy arrived, greeted the envoys, and took their respective seats. They watched female musicians and dancers and drank several round before bringing the banquet to a close. The envoys wanted to depart despite the rain, but the reception envoy said, "The rainy conditions are such that: the road ahead is muddy, much worse than previously. I dare to ask that we stay here [until conditions improve]."

The envoys replied, "If the rain does not stop, then we should stay here, but if it lets up even a little, we must depart immediately."

That evening there was another banquet. Once the banquet was over, the reception envoy went before the envoys and had Yi Hwajong tell them, "His Majesty has been sending notices everyday concerning the protocols for receiving the imperial edict. I think there may be some mistake so my fear knows no bounds. When the king holds your audience at court, there is no distance he will not go to express his reverence for you, but normally, His Majesty cannot drink alcohol. When he receives you, I am deeply concerned that his sincere intention will be clouded by some difficulty."

The envoys asked, "The king will not drink alcohol because he is receiving an imperial edict?"

The reception envoy replied, "It is not on account of this particular event, but rather it is due to his natural disposition; he cannot drink."

The envoys had Yi Hwajong say to the reception envoy, "The assistant Paek Such'ŏn 白壽千 wishes to accompany us and discuss books. Arrange for him to follow us for two or three days." The reception envoy immediately ordered that a horse be provided to Paek so he could accompany the entourage.

April 7, 1537

(2/28)

Morning clouds, afternoon rain.

The envoys departed and later arrived at Unam-wŏn 雲巖院. They

stepped down from their palanquins, seemingly with the intention of resting a while, but they abruptly got back in and were again on their way, eventually arriving at Sungnyŏng-gwan 肅寧館. They summoned the reception envoy to join them for their midday meal, after which they went up to the upper deck of the pavilion from whence they enjoyed a broad view. Finally, they departed, arriving at Anjŏng-gwan 安定館 by sunset.

Dinner was ready by nine o'clock in the evening and after two rounds of wine, it was over. The chief envoy asked Yi Hwajong, "Why is it that between here and Sukch'ŏn 肅川 there are no post stations?"

Yi Hwajong replied, "There have never been places to pitch a tent and have lunch [in this area].

"Are there no stations between here and P'yŏngyang?" the chief envoy asked.

"Pusan-wŏn 斧山院 is on the way. There will be a full tea there," Yi Hwajong replied.

April 8, 1537

(2/29)

Clear.

At seven o'clock in the morning, the envoys took their seats in the main hall and summoned the reception envoy to join them for breakfast. They then departed and arrived at Pusan-wŏn. The envoys summoned the reception envoy and together they had tea and cookies, during which time they had Yi Hwajong say to the reception envoy, "After we reach the city [of P'yŏngyang] and conduct the welcoming ceremonies for the imperial proclamation, we will go the Tomb of Kija, the Altar to Confucius, and the Tomb of Tan'gun 檀君.[34] After that we will see P'ungwŏl-lu and Yŏn'gwang-jŏng 練光亭."

Yi Hwajong said, "The Tomb of Kija is outside the city. If we enter the city and then come out again we still have to go a further ten *li*."

"If that is the case, we will have to wait until the return journey to see the Tomb of Kija."

---

34 Tan'gun was the legendary founder of the kingdom of Old Chosŏn (*Ko Chosŏn* 古朝鮮). See Iryŏn, *Chŭngbo samguk yusa*, Ch'oe Namsŏn, ed., (Sŏul: Minjung Sŏgwan, 1954), 33-34.

Ten *li* before the procession reached the walls, people from P'yŏngyang had decorated two carriages in bright colors which then preceded the envoys as the approached the city. Acrobats followed the end of the procession. Governor Yi Kwiryŏng and officials from the P'yŏngyang city government welcomed the imperial proclamation at the Pot'ong Gate (Pot'ong-mun 普通門). At one o'clock in the afternoon, the processioned entered the city, but for quite some time the envoys lingered by Pot'ong Gate to look at all the welcome decorations. Once the entourage arrived at the main hall of the P'yŏngyang administrative offices, Hospitality envoy So Seyang 蘇世讓, the governor, and sundry local officials formed themselves into two files, one to the east and one to the west, and welcomed the imperial proclamation. The envoys then took their seats in the main hall and the reception envoy and all the lower ranking officers then saluted them. The interpreter Hong Kyŏm 洪謙 arrived from Seoul and asked to permission to greet the envoys, bowing to both of them.

The envoys set out together for the Tomb of Kija but their guide misunderstood and instead took the them to the Altar to Confucius. "It would be appropriate to perform bows," the envoys said and so they performed four bows. They then went to the hall of sages (*sŏngjŏn* 聖殿), looked at the statuary, and said to the interpreter, "Your country greatly reveres the moral transformative power of scholarship. This temple is grand and we are overcome with delight."

They went on to the Tomb of Kija and bowed four times. They read the plaques and all the epigraphy within the courtyard and [the chief envoy] said, "These are good texts."[35] They also went to the Tomb of Tan'gun and saluted the plaques bearing the names of Tan'gun and King Tongmyŏng (Tongmyŏng-wang 東明王)[36] and then left. They also climbed up into Yŏn'gwang-jŏng 練光亭, Ŭpho-ru 挹灝樓, and P'ungwŏl-lu 風月樓, read all the poetry plaques, and then returned to Taedong-gwan 大同館, walking in front of the welcome decorations, looking at the clay figures (*chapsang* 雜像)[37] arranged on the hips of the rooves. They sat in the doorway of the of Taedong-gwan for a long time watching the acrobats perform. They again went up

---

35 See also Ŏ Sukkwŏn, "P'aegwan chapki," 151; Ŏ Sukkwŏn, *Storyteller's Miscellany*, 246.

36 Tongmyŏng was the posthumous name of Ko Chumong 高朱蒙, the founder of the Koguryŏ 高句麗 Kingdom. See Kim Pusik, *Samguk sagi* (Sŏul: Minjok Munhwa Ch'ujinhoe, 1973), 13:1a-5a; Iryŏn, *Chŭngbo samguk yusa*, 40-41; Kim Pusik, "Sage King Tongmyŏng" in *The Koguryŏ Annals of the Samguk Sagi*, trans. Kenneth H. J. Gardiner *et al* (Seongnam, Korea: The Academy of Korean Studies Press, 2011), 37-44.

37 There are ten such figures, representing earth spirits and characters from the Ming-era novel *Journey to the West* (K. *Sŏyu ki*, C. *Xiyou ji* 西遊記), placed on the roof hips of official buildings to protect against malevolent spirits and ill fortune. Yu Mongin 柳夢寅 relates an anecdote in which Yu Chosaeng 柳肇生, upon his appointment to high office, was compelled by his new senior colleagues to recite the names of each of the ten *chapsang* ten times in a single breath as part of his informal initiation into the bureaucracy. See Yi Nŭnghwa, *Han'guk togyo sa* (Sŏul: Tongguk Taehakkyo, 1959), 373, 377-378; Yu Mongin, *Ŏu yadam: wŏnmun* (Sŏul: Tolbegae, 2019), 206; Yu Mongin, *Ŏu yadam* trans. Sin Ikch'ŏl, Yi Hyŏngdae, Cho Yunghŭi, and No Yŏngmi (Sŏul: Tolbegae, 2019), 494.

into K'waejae-jŏng 快哉亭 and talked for a very long time. They did not return to their quarters until the early evening, whereupon they instructed the hospitality envoy to delay the welcoming banquet until the following morning. As the assistant envoy was leaving Anjŏng-gwan, he gave a small fan that he was carrying to the doorman [to keep for him]. The doorman lost it. The reception envoy had the staff search for it but they could not find it so he sent a message to the governor to find it.

The assistant envoy was in his room and wrote a note on a single sheet of paper, giving it to [the interpreter] Kim Sanhae 金山海 to deliver to the reception envoy. The note read, "You must compile of a list of the names of all the official buildings, mountains, rivers, ponds, crags, ravines, and temples in the Ŭiju area, including ruins, and their basic facts. Also list for me all the administrative districts through which we will pass on the way to the capital. In the case of Ŭiju, include notes on the pronunciation of Ŭisun-gwan 義順館, Yangch'aek-kwan 良策館, Sogok-kwan 所串館, and an explanation of the origins of their names. Do the same for mountains and rivers."

April 9, 1537

(2/30)

Clear.

At seven o'clock in the morning the envoys emerged from their quarters and took their seats in the main hall for the welcoming banquet. The host and hospitality envoys each offered wine to the envoys and then the female dancers and musicians performed. Once the banquet was completed, the reception envoy informed the envoys, "The royal reception of the imperial proclamation will be on April 18 (3/9), an auspicious day (*kiril* 吉日). This I dare to report."

"This is very good. If it rains, we shall travel to one post station. If it is clear, we shall double the pace. We must arrive in the capital by this day."

The reception envoy asked about the content of the two imperial edicts that were unrelated to Chosŏn. The envoys said, "We have already spoken of this completely. Why do you ask again? Generally, protocol dictates that once the edict has been issued, it is returned to the secretariat for archiving. We submitted a formal request [to the Board of Rites] that read, 'The edict we are carrying should be returned to the secretariat for archiving but in this case might it be acceptable to leave it [with the Chosŏn government]?' The Board of Rites received a Sagely Directive [from the throne] that read, 'If this country wishes to keep it, allow it.' And so, we have copied it onto yellow paper, and brought it with us. As for the other edict, we have been appointed envoys to a far land; how could we be without any self-control? Indeed, this is why we have been appointed envoys to deliver this Sagely Directive."

The reception envoy also asked, "As this edict is not related to our country, it is not necessary to conduct a reception ceremony [for it]. Should it be omitted from the ceremonial notes?"

"In this instance, there need not be a ritual to welcome the edict but what harm would there be if you were to include it in the protocol notes? If a ritual should not be done, it would be completely inappropriate to record it. If a ritual should be done, why get hung up on the one time it is not done and omit it from the ritual program?"

The assistant envoy summoned the interpreter and had him tell the reception envoy, "It turns out that the doorman to whom I had entrusted my fan yesterday inadvertently wrapped it up in a coat. We found it today," and then he held up the fan for all to see.

The envoys departed at nine o'clock in the morning and arrived at the official yacht on the Taedong River (Taedong-gang 大同江). As they praised the spectacular landscape of mountains and rivers, they pointed to a painting on the wall entitled, *Panorama of the City of Kija* (*Kisŏng-do* 箕城圖), "So, it seems we have here a fine painter, indeed! He's included the welcoming of the imperial proclamation yesterday, as well as a scene of us coming here and appreciating all the sights. And here the carthorses hanging their necks low, waiting to depart! It would very good if, once we get to the capital, a skilled painter makes a copy for each of us so that later we can take pleasure in appreciating our time here." They said this two or three times.

The envoys also said, "The plaques for Yŏn'gwang-jŏng and P'ungwŏl-lu are not done in regular script (*haebop* 楷法). On the way back, we will write them for you."

The governor asked them to name the official yacht and the chief envoy said, "It would be proper to call it 'Crossing the River' (Jichuan 濟川)."

Interpreter Hong Kyŏm said, "There is a pavilion by that name in the capital."

The chief envoy asked the assistant envoy to provide a new name so the assistant envoy said, "It would be fitting to name it 'Riding the Blue' (chengbi 乘碧). I will write it for you."

At one o'clock in the afternoon, the disembarked from the official yacht and took their seats beneath a small canopy on the river bank. They again called for a fisherman to cast nets and catch fish. After some time passed they departed and went to Taejŏng 大井, where the left their palanquins to look around. In the evening they reached Saengyang-gwan 生陽館 in Taehwa 大和.

As soon as they arrived, they moved to the eastern chambers and had a target set up before the front gate. Then they called for archers to shoot one round. They had an attendant set up a torch more than forty paces distant, make a target of red paper, and attach it to the torch. They commanded them to shoot. Yongch'ŏn 龍泉 Great County Magistrate (*kunsu* 郡守) Cho Sebong and the military officer from Ŭiju, Sŏ Kyŏngch'ŏn, both hit the target. The envoys also had their attendant try drawing the archers' bows. They finished by five o'clock in the evening.

The chief envoy asked Yi Hwajong, "Is there a *touhu* 投壺[38] set here?"

"There is one in P'yŏngyang."

"Bring it quickly."

The envoy also said, "Our palanquins are lined in wool but these springs days are getting warmer and warmer. Is it possible to make a lighter,

38 K. *t'uho*. This is a game in which players attempt to toss arrows into narrow holes in a vase or similar cylinder. It is in principle similar to the game cornhole.

single-layered liner?" The reception envoy issued an order to the Chunghwa County (Chunghwa-gun 中和郡) magistrate to make a single-layer liner of cobalt-blue cotton.

An octopus arrived from the capital and was presented to the chief envoy, who responded, "This is extremely peculiar. There are octopi where I am from but never have I seen anything quite like this!" The envoys retired to their quarters, ordering the banquet to be postponed to the following day.

April 10, 1537
(3/1)
Clear.

At seven o'clock in the morning the envoys emerged from the main hall and took their seats at the morning meal. Once the meal was finished, they departed and arrived at Chŏbog-wŏn 貯福院 where they had lunch and tea with the reception envoy.[39] At one o'clock in the afternoon, the entourage arrived at Hwangju 黃州. Yi Ŏkson 李億孫, governor of Hwanghae Province, along with the staff members of the local government offices, all gathered at the five-*li* point to welcome the imperial proclamation. Acrobats spun and twirled the garlands attached to the palanquins in welcome. When the entourage reached the main gate the envoys stopped the palanquins to look at the decorations and entertainment before going in to stand in the main hall. Hospitality envoy Kim Inson 金麟孫, along with the governor and the local government staff divided themselves into east and west files to perform the ceremony to receive the imperial proclamation. When this was complete they each greeted the envoys individually. The person from

39 Ŏ Sukkwŏn 魚叔權 writes that guesthouses were often given colloquial names that arose locally and organically, largely because, as Ŏ would have it, Korean people were not terribly fond of working and did not want to take the effort to come up with loftier formal names. In this case, the name of the guesthouse was Chŏbokchi 貯卜只, the colloquial place name rendered phonetically in Sino-Korean characters, meant only to be read phonetically, not semantically. When Gong Yongqing, the chief envoy, asked Chŏng Saryong, the reception envoy, what the name of the guesthouse was, Chŏng did not want to have to explain the colloquial name, or its phonetic rendering, so he improvised on the spot and changed *bok* from 卜 to 福, thereby changing the meaning to the effect of "gathering good fortune." Gong was so moved by the name that he wrote a poem, "In the Three Han, steep mountains surround the post road, only in fields does fortune gather," meant to evoke the scene of the guesthouse nestled among the mountains. In this instance, "Three Han" (Sanhan三韓) is a poetic archaism indicating the Korean peninsula. A plaque was mounted with the new name and the poem, thereby, in Ŏ Sukkwŏn's words, "saving the guesthouse, just barely, from its provincialism." See Ŏ Sukkwŏn, "P'aegwan chapki," 151; Ŏ Sukkwŏn, *Storyteller's Miscellany*, 244. For the original name of the guesthouse, see No Sasin et al., comp., *Sinjŭng tongguk yŏji sŭngnam* (Sŏul: Myŏngmundang, 1994), 41:7b; Kim Chŏngho, *Taedong chiji* (Sŏul: Hanyang Taehakkyo pusŏl Kukhak Yŏn'guwŏn, 1974), 18:3b.

P'yŏngyang with the *t'uho* set arrived and the envoys sat together in the eastern chambers and played several rounds. At the welcoming banquet that evening, the hospitality envoy, the reception envoy, and governor all made toasts. The hospitality envoy wanted to do another round but the envoys said, "We are both exhausted and do not need to drink again. Let us meet again on the Han River (Han-gang 漢江) in the capital."

April 11, 1537

(3/2)

Clear.

The envoys departed and later arrived at Ŏch'o River (*Ŏch'o-ch'ŏn* 於草川) where they boarded an official yacht. They called the reception envoy to join them and together they drank a little and had some fish caught. There was quite a variety of fish and in each case [the envoys] asked for their Korean names and then provided them in Chinese. They also ordered the fish to be cooked and served but, the chief envoy saw that when the fish were ready, none was served to the reception envoy or the governor.

He asked why. The reception envoy had the interpreter say, "Today is the anniversary of the passing of a previous king. The local officials have vowed to forego meat and side dishes on this day."

"Your state ritual operates in very much the same way as the [Ming] court. If the [Ming] court continues for ten-thousand years, your state, too, will continue for ten-thousand years."

The chief envoy asked the assistant envoy to name the river and the official yacht. The assistant envoy named the river "Exquisite Silk Stream" (Cujin-xi 簇錦溪) and named the yacht "Distant Cloud" (Yaoyun 搖雲). The chief envoys said to the reception envoy, "The level of the culture and reverent ritual courtesies of your country is similar to those of the Central Court (Zhongchao 中朝).[40] What regions beyond the seas could compare? Both of us continually sigh in astonishment." He also said, "On the road ahead, we wish to go and appreciate all the beautiful mountains and outstanding rivers that our eyes can take in. Surely, minister, you know this!"

At one o'clock in the afternoon, they departed and reached Kŭksŏng-wŏn 棘城院 where they rested briefly before resuming the journey. After just a few *li*, the envoys descended from their palanquins and climbed to

40 This is a reference to the Ming court.

a hilltop from whence they could see the sea directly. Once they arrived at Sari-wŏn 沙里院, they had lunch. The chief envoy instructed Yi Hwajong to say, "This place is close to the sea so, if the oysters and clams are fresh and delicious, it would be good to get some."

The assistant envoy said, "Grandfather Gong lives on the coast and is thoroughly familiar with all the flavors of the sea and every kind of fresh fish. Tell the minister to serve seafood repeatedly."

At five o'clock in the evening, they arrived at Pongsan 鳳山. The chief envoy said, "Today we are exhausted. You may postpone the banquet until tomorrow morning." He then walked to a thatched pavilion among the pines and summoned the assistant envoy and together they walked in the pine shade. They returned under blossoming pear trees where they played *t'uho*, joking with one another. They then they drank together until nine o'clock in the evening (*igyŏng* 二更) when they finally stopped.

The chief envoy summoned Yi Hwajong and asked him, "Is there anyone among the current retinue who was assigned to accompany Tang and Shi when they were here?"

Yi Hwajong knew that the envoy was asking this after having read the *Brilliant Flowers Anthology* and so he replied, "The current reception envoy Minister Chŏng and the hospitality envoy in P'yŏngyang, Minister So, were both assigned to the [reception] commission at that time."

The chief envoy asked, "At that time, who was the director of the royal household supplies?" He likely asked because the reception envoy had been the director of the royal household supplies at that time.

April 12, 1537

(3/3)

Clear.

The envoys finished the meal at the lodgings at seven o'clock in the morning and then went to their separate rooms. The reception envoy and the governor spoke with one another and then instructed Yi Hwajong to ask the envoys, "Today is the third day of the third month. It is this custom of this land to make mugwort pastries (*aebyŏng* 艾餠) and have a mountaintop picnic. On the top of the mountain to the south of the guesthouse, there is a thatched pavilion. It is the highest spot in the area and one can see great distances from there. Perhaps we might stay a while and do this?"

The envoys said, "Permitted." And so, the entourage went to the mountaintop and the envoys sat together with the reception envoy and the governor in the thatched pavilion. They drank a little wine and had the archers shoot targets. The chief envoy repeatedly offered the governor a large cup of wine, but only a medium cup of wine to the reception envoy and said, "Today I want to see how much you can drink!" Then he gave wine to the archers. And then he called the attendants, doctors, and all the staff and gave them wine, too.

As the hour grew late, the entourage departed and later arrived at Kŏmsu-gwan 釰水館 where they had lunch. Protocol Inquiry Officer Im P'irhyŏng had already arrived the night before. The entourage spent the night there.

In accordance with a royal command that had arrived from the capital, the reception envoy made an inquiry of the envoys. They replied, "We have brought edicts with us that we copied onto yellow paper with the permission of the emperor, but they are related only to our embassy and have no relation to your country. With the issuance of an edict, we send the staff whom we bring with us ahead to the official guest house. [The edicts we carry] instruct us not to burden the Chosŏn security detail with the staff whom we send ahead." They also said, "The edict [issued to Chosŏn] is of a different character than usual in that the emperor has personally composed it. The margins of the text are adorned with golden dragons. The Elder of the Hall (*gelao* 閣老),[41] Li Shi 李時, said to us, 'Never have I seen an edict of such exceptional favor.' When the king opens and reads this edict, he will surely know the deep love of [our] court and leap with delight." Normally, protocol requires that once the king reads the edict, he must return it. We have received instructions, however, to deal with the edict as the king wishes, whether he would like to return it or keep it. Should he elect to keep it, it would truly be a treasure that secures the country. It would be absolutely inappropriate to divulge the content of the edict before [the king] opens and reads it."

The reception envoy asked if the wine protocols for this part of the itinerary were to differ in any way from those in the ceremonial notes. The envoys replied, "As for the wine protocols, you should enact them as usual. When your country enacts these protocols, it should be according to its own old rules. It would be appropriate to use the same ceremonial notes used for Chancellor Tang."

The protocol inquiry officer met with the envoys and said, "The ritual of five bows and three prostrations is not recorded in the ceremonial notes

41 This is an informal term for "grand secretary" (*daxueshi* 大學士).

of the Hongwu 洪武 reign and later courts did not issue any other special editions. Our country has followed the old protocols for generations; they must not be changed in haste."

The envoys replied, "This ritual is standard ritual practiced throughout the world. It cannot be omitted. Your country always speaks of its reverent practice of the ways of civilization, but if you have not practiced this kind of standard ritual, just what sort of ritual is it that you have been practicing? Protocols for the issuance of edicts did not exist only during the Hongwu reign. [The imperial court] frequently issued them during the Yongle 永樂 and Xuande 宣德 reigns as well. Has your country not overlooked something as it has researched old precedents? Has your research into precedents made the mistake of drawing upon the Hongwu period exclusively? In the case of this edict, when the king opens and reads it, he will certainly give rise to a desire to welcome the loving concern of the [imperial] court and to a heart of sincere reverence. Because our discussion has been through translators, it seems that there yet remain some issues not fully conveyed. It would thus be appropriate for me to provide for you a written explanation." The chief envoy then wrote out the protocols for welcoming the edict outside the walls of the capital and gave the document to the protocol inquiry officer. His text reads as follows:

I have spoken with the protocol officers concerning ceremonies for several days now and I fear that the interpreters have not been fully accurate so I will take up this matter personally to explain it. Presently, princes and the entirety of their officials welcome imperial proclamations outside the walls of their capitals. First they must perform the five bows and three prostrations. Once this is complete, the embassy proceeds to enter the country. And then at each local government office, the proclamation is opened and read, in accordance with the ceremonial notes prepared by your protocol officers one day in advance. In regard to the question of reducing or eliminating elements of these ceremonies, we are not suggesting any changes to existing protocols but rather we are only insisting on complete protocols. Moreover, this is the standard protocol throughout the world. If your country alone does not do it, then there are two different bodies of ceremonial practice. This is a proclamation from the one emperor and we are all the same subjects of the one emperor. How could there be two sets of ceremonial practice [one for you and one for everyone else]? As we have passed through each place on our itinerary over the last few days, the minister, second minister, and the governor have all been on the side of the road bowing. There is a problem we have not taken up, however, and that is the fact that we have not yet opened the imperial proclamation and read it. And now we have already arrived in your country. Is it acceptable for your king to perform this ceremony now, like this? If it is as you say, your king does not have an advance guard. But there are the three stamps of the feet and three claps of the hands (*sanwudao* 三舞蹈) [in salute from your officials]. And there are already twelve bows. Why is it that it is only this ceremony outside the capital walls that you hate and will not do? The other rituals have all been done. Only this one you do not do. One can say you are omitting the important in favor of the trifling. This is the first time an imperial proclamation has arrived [from this emperor] and the beginning of your king's contact [with this emperor], so it is all the more important that you execute all the rituals completely. In this way you make the people of this country understand that your king fully reveres the imperial court. Only then will your people know what it means to fully revere your country. In matters of beauty such as this, I would not lead you to fail to execute the rituals [properly]. The Son of Heaven treats your king as he would any other in the world and yet, the conduct of ritual in your country is somehow different from anywhere else in the world. This is an exception you have made on your own. We have heard that your king is worthy and that your country maintains ritual and righteousness. Since we arrived at the frontier, everything has been done flawlessly so we do not hold back on this one word. Go back to your king and tell him that if he should only seek peace of mind then the ritual seems fitting. What we are saying is not a matter of being argumentative or contrarian, nor is it something unreasonable. It would just be regrettable to us if your country that places so much importance on ritual were to do it incorrectly. Today we hear that your country has commanded that the classics licentiates of each place on our itinerary welcome the imperial proclamation and we are

> extremely pleased. This is not something that a country that maintains ritual and righteousness can fail to do. When the [imperial] court hears of this, it will surely be deeply pleased and its care and consideration for your country will grow by the day.[42]

At three o'clock in the afternoon, the envoys ascended to the deck of the gate house to see the distant views. As the light grew dim, they announced that they would retire to their quarters and ordered the banquet to be postponed until the following day.

April 13, 1537

(3/4)

Clear.

At nine o'clock in the morning, the envoys took their seats in the main

42 This text, albeit with minor differences, can be found in Gong Yongqing's *Shi chaoxian lu* 使朝鮮錄. See Kong Yonggyŏng, *Sa chosŏn rok* (Sŏul: Han'guk Kojŏn Kanhaenghoe, 1975), 2:89a-90b. The debate was extended and blunt. It centered around two issues in the ceremonies for welcoming the imperial proclamation: the five bows and three prostrations to the proclamation and the gathering of the local classics licentiates to welcome the proclamation. See Kong Yonggyŏng, *Sa Chosŏn rok* 2:90b-94a.

hall. As they took their morning meal, they said to the reception envoy, "Having read the *Brilliant Flowers Anthology*, it appears that the landscape of the South River (*Nam-gang* 南江) at Yongch'ŏn-gwan 龍泉館 is quite remarkable. When Expositor-in-Waiting (*shijiang* 侍講) Dong Yue 董越 was here, he watched a pheasant hunt and wrote a poem to record it.[43] Today we should go beyond Ch'ongsu Mountain. We do not have much time and cannot tarry long, but let us wait just a little while and have some tea before we go."

The reception envoy said, "The governor of this province has already arranged a place and set up a tent."

After the meal, the envoys went directly to South River where they strolled and watched the water. After a long while they sat down and called for tea. They drank a round of tea and then called for wine, saying, "We originally only intended to drink tea, but Grandfather Wu[44] asked to drink three cups of wine so we have called for wine." They also spoke quietly to the reception envoy, "Is it not fortunate that we have been able to follow in

---

43 Dong Yue was the chief Ming envoy in 1488. While it is not entirely clear which poem or poems Gong cites here, there are two that Dong wrote at Yongch'ŏn-gwan, one of which features the cry of a pheasant. See Hwanghwa chip (Sŏul: Ch'ŏngun Munhwasa, 1994), 10:24b, 12:8a. See also, No Sasin et al., *Sinjŭng Tongguk yŏji sŭngnam*, 41:23b.

44 This is assistant envoy Wu Ximeng.

the very footsteps of our predecessors who enjoyed this very spot?" before departing.

The entourage arrived at Ansŏng-gwan 安城館 at eleven o'clock in the morning and had lunch. They then continued quickly on to Ch'ongsu Mountain. The envoys walked up to the stele inscription by Expositor-in-Waiting Dong and read it several times, unable to suppress their repeated sighs. They turned to Yi Hwajong and asked, "Why hasn't your king had a structure built to protect this stele from the elements? It would be but a small expense. Moreover, why is there so much damage to the face of the stele?"

Yi Hwajong replied, "Ignorant woodsmen thoughtlessly struck it and caused this damage.[45] Our majesty commanded that the guilty party be arrested and punished. There is now only a temporary fence to protect the stele."

After they were finished reading the inscription, they went back down to the riverside, and in the tent, they changed into causal clothes and shoes.

---

45 According to Ŏ Sukkwŏn, an "ignorant passerby" (無識往來者) thought that the Chinese, being deeply learned in geomancy, had placed the stele in this location specifically to suppress Chosŏn, which, to the passerby, explained the then-current crop failure. He took a stone and repeatedly struck it against the stele, managing to obliterate twenty or thirty percent of the text. See, Ŏ Sukkwŏn, "P'aegwan chapki," 151. O Sukkwŏn, *Storyteller's Miscellany*, 243.

They again walked up and down the river bank repeatedly. Crossing the water on a single log, they became so transfixed by watching the water pass through the stones below that they forgot to return.

The governor brought a variety of fresh seafood, including several kinds of large and small oysters. The chief envoy was delighted to see them and took a plate of the small oysters. He had an attendant roast them in their shells before the entourage. And then he summoned the reception envoy and the governor, and had them sit on the ground. The chief envoy got up himself and took a small oyster, opened it with a little knife he had, and ate it. With each one he ate, he praised the flavor. He opened and ate until he filled his plate with empty shells. He then laughed and shared the remaining oysters with the reception envoys and the governor, "Gentleman, it is funny that high officials such as yourselves live in a land that produces oysters and yet you do not know how to roast and eat them!"

After they drank four or five rounds of wine and put their cups down, the chief envoy said, "Our house is on the seashore and we eat these quite frequently. My hometown is 8,000 *li* from the imperial capital. Now, having come east, I am more than 10,000 *li* from home. How could it not be fated that we should enjoy one another's company in this moment?"

The assistant envoy said, "Fujian 福建 is on the shore of the great ocean and is in close contact with Liuqiu 琉球 and Zhancheng 占城.[46] My hometown is Changzhou 常州, on banks of the Yangzi River (Yangzi-jiang 揚子江). It takes more than one month to travel to Fujian from there."

Local officials called on their falconers to release their falcons. They chased a pheasant, caught it, and dropped it before the entourage. They also caught a live deer. The envoys could not contain their delight.

The envoys reached Posan-gwan 寶山館 at sunset and, before reaching their quarters, they got out of their palanquins, changed their clothing, and went in. They ordered that the banquet be postponed until the following day.

April 14, 1537

(3/5)

Clear.

Zhang Quan 張全, an attendant of the chief envoy, was sixteen

46 This refers to the kingdom once located in southern Vietnam, Chiêm Thành 占城, also known as Chăm Pa 占婆.

years old. He tried in jest to take the belt from one of the Posan-gwan gatekeepers.[47] Because they both grabbed at the belt at the same time, the staff that the gatekeeper was holding accidentally made contact with Zhang Quan's head. Zhang said, "This gatekeeper struck me!" and then later told the chief envoy. The reception envoy heard this and commanded Yi Rim 李霖, the P'yŏngsan magistrate, to detain and question the gatekeeper and then administer severe punishment. The gatekeeper was thus fettered and detained in the courtyard. At seven o'clock in the morning, the chief envoy emerged and took his seat in the main hall where he ate his meal. Once he was done he summoned the gatekeeper and said, "If you really did strike Zhang Quan, it would not be a light crime, but I just heard the two of you joking with one another, so it is clear that you did not intend to strike him." The chief envoy ordered his release.

At nine o'clock in the morning, the envoys departed and later arrived at a small pavilion in front of the P'yŏngsan Magistracy offices. They descended from their palanquins and sat down in the pavilion where they ate a brief meal and quickly departed, arriving at Kŭmam-gwan 金巖館, where they had lunch. The chief envoy had Yi Hwajong ask the reception

---

47 For an alternate translation of this passage, see Chŏng, *Ch'ŏnsa illo ilgi*, 65.

envoy, "Yesterday we saw an unusually steep and jagged peak just to the east of Ch'ongsu Mountain, and far more impressive. What is it called?"

The reception envoy replied, "Our country has many mountains; those comparable to this are countless. How could they all have names? In colloquial parlance, [the mountains in that area] are called 'Ch'ongsu Mountain' collectively."

At three o'clock in the afternoon, the envoys arrived at Chŏt'an 猪灘.[48] They descended from their palanquins and sat in a tent at the riverside wherein they had a few rounds of wine. The governor presented them with several kinds of seafood and they thanked him. They then boarded the official yacht and crossed the river. As night fell, they reached Hŭngŭi-gwan 興義館 and ordered the banquet to be postponed until the following day. The chief envoy had his meal and then, as he watched the various staff [performing their duties], he pointed to the Prefect of Changyŏn (Changyŏn hyŏn'gam 長連縣監), Sŏng Ch'ŏlmun 成哲文, and asked about his background. Kim Haesan replied, "He is a legacy appointment (*munŭm* 門蔭)."

"What is a legacy appointment?" the chief envoy asked.

---

48 Chŏt'an is located on the upper reaches of the Yesŏng River (*Yesŏng-gong* 禮成江) in Hwanghae Province.

"His grandfather[49] was third censor (*hŏnnap* 獻納) in the Office of the Censor-General (*Saganwŏn* 司諫院) and highly accomplished in remonstrance so [the state] appoints his descendants to office [to this day]."

The chief envoy replied, "This truly is a great system!"

The reception envoy had the interpreter report to the envoys that light palanquins (*yanggyo* 涼轎) [more appropriate for warmer weather] would soon be sent. The envoys were pleased.

In the early evening, the assistant envoy summoned Kim Sanhae and said, "Grandfather Gong[50] could not stop sighing his praises of the peak across from Ch'ongsu Mountain so he named it "Azure Screen" (*cuiping* 翠屏) and wrote a poem about it. Only you know so please do not tell the minister."

---

49 The grandfather is likely Sŏng Han 成翰, third censor in the Office of the Censor-General from September 1501 to March 1502. His career seems to have come to an end after a chance street encounter with Yi Hang 李恒, Prince Anyang (Anyang-gun 安陽君). The prince was accompanied by a single servant so Sŏng assumed the prince was merely another official and demanded that both he and the prince dismount and salute one another as peers. Sŏng later realized his transgression and confessed, but only to not making way for the prince, not to demanding that the prince dismount. The prince himself later provided a more complete account of the incident, moving the sovereign Prince Yŏnsan (Yŏnsan-gun 燕山君) to command that Sŏng be subject to interrogation by the Office of the Censor-General. After the interrogation, Sŏng vanished from the records of state without even a mention of his dismissal. A new third censor, Sin Ching 申澄, was appointed two weeks after the interrogation. As interrogations often involved physical torture, it is not unreasonable to suspect that Sŏng may have died as a result of the investigation. See *Yŏnsan-gun ilgi* 7/8/8; 8/1/24; 8/1/25; 8/2/9.

50 This is the chief envoy Gong Yongqing.

April 15, 1537

(3/6)

Clear.

The envoys took their seats in the main hall and had their meal. At nine o'clock in the morning, they got into their light palanquins and departed, arriving at Ojo River (Ojo-ch'ŏn 吾助川). They descended from their palanquins and looked around, saying, "Among all the mountains and rivers through which we have passed so far, nothing has looked quite as beautiful as this. On the way back, we must stop here for a little while before moving on." They also said to Yi Hwajong, "The light palanquins in which we now ride are quite beautiful."

Hwajong said, "His Majesty was concerned about the lined palanquins under the hot sun and so especially commanded that these be made and sent [for your use]."

The envoys looked at one another in astonishment and said, "How considerate is the king to have thought even of this! Summon the porters [who brought them] here. We wish to think them personally."

Yi Hwajong replied, "The porters returned last night as soon as they had replaced the palanquins."

At eleven o'clock in the morning, the entourage arrived at Kŭmgyo-gwan 金郊館. The envoys stood in the main hall and saw that two sections of the windscreen were painted with scenes of the Hwanghang-nu 黃鶴樓 and Koso-dae 姑蘇臺. And they asked, "Where in your country are these places?"

Interpreter Hong Kyŏm 洪謙 replied, "These pavilions are in Kyŏngsang Province (Kyŏngsang-do 慶尚道).

The chief envoy said, "I hear that the minister's hometown is in Tongnae Prefecture (Tongnae-hyŏn 東萊縣) in Kyŏngsang Province, where the mountains and rivers are of exceptional beauty. Is this not a picture of that place?"

"It is."

The envoys pointed out the features of the drawing for some time and then said, "This really is a fine landscape."

The reception envoy had Yi Hwajŏng tell the envoys, "We will spend tonight at [the offices of] the Kaesŏng Magistracy (Kaesŏng-bu 開城府). The night of April 17 (3/7) will be in Tongp'a 東坡. On April 18 (3/8) we will be in Pyŏkche-gwan 碧蹄館. On April 19 (3/9), we will enter the capital. This is the route that lies ahead and this is the itinerary I have dared to report."

The envoys replied, "We already know the itinerary, and it is appropriate to proceed as you have suggested."

The envoys departed after lunch and later arrived at the Sanye Post Station (Sanye-yŏk 狻猊驛). The Kaesŏng Magistracy had erected a tent on a high hill by the side of the road. The envoys descended from their palanquins and rested briefly with tea. As soon as they had finished, they again departed, later arriving at Yŏngbin-gwan 迎賓館. The Governor of Kyŏnggi Province Kim Hŭiyŏl 金希說, Inspector Yi Tang 李塘, Kaesŏng Magistrate Han Yunch'ang 韓允昌, Secretary (*sŭngji* 承旨) An U 安宇, Inspector Kim Hwak 金擴, and other local magistrates and staff welcomed the imperial proclamation in front of Yŏngbin-gwan.

At three o'clock in the afternoon, the entourage entered the office compound. Hospitality envoy Yu Serin 柳世麟, Special Hospitality Envoy Pak Suryang 朴守良, and various local magistrates and miscellaneous officials divide into eastern and western files and then conducted the welcoming ceremony for the imperial proclamation. Later, the reception envoy, the hospitality envoy, and other officials personally greeted the envoys and then left.

The envoys said, "We are exhausted from the activities today so it would be best to postpone the welcoming banquet until tomorrow morning." That evening, the assistant envoy took hot water into his chambers and bathed.

April 16, 1537
(3/7)
Clear.

At seven o'clock in the morning, the welcoming banquet was set in the main hall. The envoys emerged and took their seats. The reception envoy, Yu Serin, Han Yunch'ang, Kim Hŭiyŏl, Pak Suryang, and others sat together along the west wall. Female entertainers (*kisaeng* 妓生) and musicians performed in front. The envoys said, "We have been busy, so you always dispense with the wine ceremonies, and yet you supply female performers (*yŏak* 女樂)?"

Pak Suryang stepped forward and had the interpreter say to the envoys, "His Majesty has especially dispatched his closest officials here together so it was necessary to augment the provisions of the banquet. If you refuse them now, it will truly forsake the feelings of His Majesty."

The envoys replied, "Since they are already here, have them perform, but from now on, when there are to be female performers, you must inform us in advance."

Pak Suryang approached the envoys and offered cups of wine in welcome, followed by Yu Serin. At this point, the envoys said, "The hour is late and there is much to do. Gentlemen, do not employ the usual ritual. Just offer a single cup of wine."

When the banquet was over, Pak Suryang approached the envoys and said, "You have sent your request [to the Ming court] and already received an answer concerning our keeping the proclamation [here in Chosŏn]. We hope that once the proclamation has been read, you leave it in the royal palace."

The envoys replied, "This request certainly shows the sincerity of your king and is worthy of being honored. When we arrive at Pyŏkche 碧蹄 we will meet with [your] senior officials, consider the situation, and then inform you [of our decision]."

The envoys returned to their chambers but soon came back out and stood together in the main hall and summoned the reception envoy, the two hospitality envoys, the governor and had them wait. They produced a text and said, "This text contains the orders we received from the emperor in their entirety. This is not a matter of our wishing to take these orders and report them to the king. We wish [instead] that you read them carefully and then simply relay their contents [to the king]." When they had finished speaking, the two hospitality envoys took their leave. The envoys then said, "The dispatch of high ministers to keep us company here is a manifestation of the sincerity of your worthy king. Thank you, thank you."

The text contained three separate official documents.

The first document:

> Minister of Rites Xia Yan 夏言 submits a memorial in reference to the Occasion of Great Joy:[51]
>
> "On October 20, 1536, we met with reverence the birth of the imperial heir apparent. As precedent dictates a proclamation of the birth to the world, this ministry submitted a memorial to the throne and received an imperial rescript approving the proposal to issue the proclamation on November 19, one month after the birth. In addition to our pleasure in this obedience, the emperor personally instructed us, 'When the crown prince was first born, we already issued a proclamation to the world, but why is it that in the case of foreign states, we do not initiate the dispatch

51 The Occasion of Great Joy (*daqingshi* 大慶事) refers to the birth of the crown prince.

of envoys to deliver the proclamation until the day of his formal investiture? Moreover, we have already informed the spirits of the world, so it would be appropriate to ensure that all know completely. And when the day of investiture comes, send another proclamation. Your Excellency shall engage in discussions and make these arrangements. Then on the nineteenth of next month, issue the proclamation of the birth of the crown prince, but not after the formal investiture of the crown prince. In accordance with precedent, dispatch one officer from the Hanlin Academy, as the chief envoy, and also one supervising secretary, as the assistant envoy, to take the proclamation to the countries of Chosŏn and Annam and inform them. On the day of the formal investiture, send envoys again to deliver the proclamation. Wait for my command to your ministry and then carry it out.' We respected the sagely command and rightly took its implementation as our order."

The Board of Rites memorialized the throne on the subject of the Occasion of Great Joy and received the sagely command, "Those appointed to go and bestow silk upon the king [of Chosŏn] are Senior Compiler Gong Yongqing of the Hanlin Academy and Supervising Secretary Wu Ximeng of the Office of Scrutiny for Revenue."

The second document:

Senior Compiler Gong Yongqing and others of the Hanlin

Academy and other offices submit a memorial in reference to the Occasion of Great Joy:

"We have humbly accepted the charge to act as chief and assistant envoys to take the proclamation to Chosŏn and inform the king so that he may know that the heart of the emperor takes all in the Six Spheres[52] as a single family, and that the moral transformation [of the emperor] that expands across the Nine States[53] and beyond without discrimination[54] is flourishing greatly. As we are about to depart and deliver the proclamation, we have a concern. If, upon arrival in that country, the intention of the king (surname, given name)[55] to revere the [Ming] throne is born of sincerity and he asks to keep the proclamation as a treasure that secures the country, then even though that sincerity, reverent of civilization and bent toward moral transformation, places the greatest of importance on ritual propriety, we would not dare on our own initiative to transfer [the proclamation to him] without a direct order. If we were to submit a memorial on this question when we meet the king, it would be a month before we would receive a reply; we would not be able to avoid

52 *Liuhe* 六合. The Six Spheres are heaven, earth, north, east, south, and west.

53 Jiuzhou 九州. When the legendary ruler Yu 禹 set about ordering his realm, he divided it into nine states. This is a term that has come to represent the central state (*chungguo* 中國). See Zou Shengmai, comp., *Shujing beizhi*, (n.p.: 1886), 2:1a-1b; Zou Shengmai, comp., *Shujing beizhi*, (Shanghai: Huiwentang Shuju, 1904), 2:1a; Namgung Chun, ed., *Sŏjŏn ku t'ohae*, (Kyŏngsŏng: Yuil Sŏgwan, 1912), 63-4.

54 The phrase in the original is *wuwai zhi hua* 無外之化.

55 The text does not indicate the surname and given name of the Chosŏn king but only the words "surname, given name" (*xinghui* 姓諱).

misunderstandings. For this reason, we submit this memorial in advance in order to ignorantly beg for an edict to this board[56] allowing us to honor the king's request to keep [the proclamation] on the basis of the precedent of the mission of Senior Compiler Lun Wenxu 倫文敍 and Junior Compiler Shen Dao 沈燾 to Annam during the Zhengde 正德 period.[57] Trusting that the great law of the court is respectfully obeyed and the hearts of the people of the outer states are faithful, we submit this memorial."

We received the sagely command, "The Ministry of Rites shall consider this and advise."

The third document:

The Ministry of Rites submits a memorial in reference to the Occasion of Great Joy:

"We have examined the text of Senior Compiler Gong Yongqing and others of the Hanlin Academy and other offices that read, in effect, 'In taking the proclamation to Chosŏn and informing the king, we fear that the king will request to keep the proclamation. We humbly ask to honor his request to keep [the proclamation] on the basis of the

56 This refers to the Ming Board of Rites.

57 The Zhengde period lasted from 1506 to 1521, so the Annam precedent was relatively recent.

> precedent of Senior Compiler Lun Wenxu and Junior Compiler Shen Dao during the Zhengde period.' We have examined the precedent in question and held discussions as to how to approach [the proposal]. When, at the proper time, the command comes down [from the throne], this ministry will execute it. Each officer agreed that in this particular instance, if the intention of the king is sincere, then it is appropriate to conform to his sentiment and honor his request to keep [the proclamation]. Because this is related to the Occasion of Great Joy and we received the order, 'The Ministry of Rites shall consider this and advise,' we now respectfully ask for a command [in response to our proposal], as in this situation, we dare not act on our own initiative."
>
> We received the sagely command, "[Do] this."

The envoys also had Yi Hwajong ask, "As for the matter of the [local] scholars' welcome of the proclamation, the protocol inquiry officer already explained that all had been set. This office is an important place so why did the scholars not come out to welcome the proclamation?"

The reception envoy replied, "The scholars' welcome of the proclamation was not normally done in the past. Now, due to Your Excellency's command, we have specially ordered it. In this instance, however, the ceremonial notes were not yet provided so the local scholars did not come to welcome the proclamation. The scholars of the national academy will, of course, welcome the proclamation."

At eleven o'clock in the morning, the entourage arrived at Ch'ohyŏn-wŏn 招賢院. The envoys summoned the reception envoy and the governor to eat together with them. The reception envoy said, "Earlier emperors personally wrote the content of their proclamations [to Chosŏn]. Were there any differences from the proclamations issued within the empire?"

The chief envoy replied, "How could I know about the content of those proclamations in any detail? When they arrived at the Grand Secretariat, I was able to see the drafts briefly. They are generally the same as the birth proclamation for all the regions, with maybe only minor differences in wording."

The reception envoy also asked, "In the memorial from the Board of Rites, there was some discussion about Chosŏn and Annam being fully informed. Is there no plan to send envoys to Annam as well?"

The envoys replied, "Although the first memorial from the Board of Rites did include that language, there is a rebellion underway in that country, so a second draft suspended the mission. As for gifts on the present mission, the Elders of the Hall discussed the matter and told us, 'Only discuss the Occasion of Great Joy; gifts are not necessary. When there is a proclamation of investiture, there will be the awarding of gifts.'"

Protocol Inquiry Officer Im P'irhyŏng brought the revised ceremonial notes and reported to the envoys, "The ceremony of the five bows and three prostrations outside the capital walls was not originally a part of the Hongwu-era ceremonies for the delivery of a proclamation so there was no preparation of such protocols before this embassy arrived. Presently, Your Excellencies have indicated that [the three bows and five prostrations] are in practice throughout the world and so wish to order their execution. His Majesty, in special deference to the words of Your Excellency, has had the protocols revised and sent presently."

The envoys replied, "Thank you so much. Your worthy king understands the importance of ritual."

At five o'clock in the evening, the envoys arrived at Tongp'a-gwan 東坡館. The chief envoy ordered Yi Hwajong to say, "We have written [poems] about all the mountains, rivers, and pavilions we have praised along the way. When we arrive at the capital, it would be good to copy them and display them on several blank scrolls.[58] They should be long and wide and make

58 The chief envoy, in fact, had asked for wooden plaques to be prepared, but the interpreter Yi Hwajong misunderstood and had an order put out for blank scrolls. When the envoys arrived in Seoul, they were presented with ten empty scrolls each. Thinking that their Chosŏn hosts were asking for samples of their calligraphy, they happily wrote out their poems from the journey on the scrolls and left. When the embassy was returning, it once again stopped at Tongp'a-gwan where Ŏ Sukkwŏn, who was then a diplomatic drafting officer in the Office of Diplomatic Correspondence and a member of the Chosŏn entourage, shared sleeping

sure to have them made quickly. Although we will only stay three days, it will be enough time to make them." He also said, "Be sure not to forget the *Panorama of P'yŏngyang* (P'yŏngyang-do 平壤圖) I requested earlier."

Dinner was served at sunset. The envoys said, "The room is narrow; do not bring the tables. Just briefly serve some wine." Once the meal was over, the reception envoy reported to the envoys the auspicious hour (*kilsi* 吉時) [for the bestowal of the proclamation] he had received from His Majesty. They replied, "We should leave at sunrise."

The reception envoy then pleaded, "If we depart at sunrise, I fear we will not arrive by the auspicious hour for the bestowal of the proclamation."

"Well then, we shall depart at three o'clock in the morning, sharp."

The chief envoy produced a document which he gave to the interpreter, and said, "As for the matter of the bestowal of proclamations to Annam, I fear the interpreter was unable to write it down [well] so I have

---

quarters with the interpreter Hong Kyŏm. They called for a lamp so they could work on the compilation of the log (呼燈撰次日記). It seems probable that this was the draft of the reception commission travel log, *Ch'ŏnsa illo ilgi*. Hong noticed the phrase "make many blank scrolls" (多造空簇) in the draft text and said, "I heard what he said; it was "plaque (*hyŏnp'an* 懸板), not blank scroll (*kongjok* 空簇)." Ŏ later confirmed this with the chief envoy himself. If indeed Ŏ was compiling the travel log, Hong would have been commenting on a draft of this very passage. See, Ŏ Sukkwŏn, "P'aegwan chapki," 137; Ŏ Sukkwŏn, *Storyteller's Miscellany*, 174. For Ŏ's title and presence in the Chosŏn entourage, see *Chungjong sillok* 32/4/30. For King Chungjong's command to provide the twenty blank scrolls, see *Chungjong sillok* 32/3/11.

written it out for you." The text read:

> I will write what I said because it will be easier to understand than communicating through the interpreter. The dispatch of envoys to your country is in all cases born of the sagely intent of the court and does not originate in past precedent. As for the previous discussion of using the standard ritual for your king, it is correct. [Our court] wished to send envoys both to your country and to Annam but later the Board of Rites considered the situation and delayed [the mission to Annam], saying 'In Annam there is now a rebellion and they have not sent tribute for several years. It is best to send special envoys to inquire as to the conditions [there].' Therefore, [the court] has only sent envoys to your country. Under these circumstances, [our court] did not send officers from the Hanlin Academy or the Offices of Scrutiny [to Annam], but rather sent two commanders from the Imperial Bodyguard to go to that country and investigate the conditions there and report back accordingly. This issue is not related to your country so we have not come to deliver any such documentation. However, the passage in the text of the memorial from the Board of Rites concerning gifts is something we have already discussed. When we were going to depart [for Chosŏn], we received an audience at court. The emperor was at Wenhua-dian 文華殿 and summoned the Grand Secretary and the Board of Rites to personally explain this matter. [Expressing his] Sagely Will, [the emperor] said, "This proclamation is only to inform the world in uniform

fashion of the birth of the imperial crown prince and is different from the matter of investiture and its related issues." In reference to the requested gifts in the memorial from the Board of Rites, the emperor replied only that they would be sent in a separate mission. This term "separate mission" means that it is expected [at a later date]. In short, the Sagely Will is that after some time, once the imperial crown prince receives investiture, there will be a separate bestowal [of gifts]. This was the main point.

When I opened and read ceremonial notes today, I sighed out loud and said, "Is this not the country that values ritual propriety and righteousness?" I once heard about Duke Huan of Qi (Qi Huan-gong 齊桓公). When the King of Zhou 周 convened a meeting at Kuiqiu 葵丘, he sent sacrificial meat to the princes and lieges. A royal messenger carried out the command [and delivered the sacrificial meat to Duke Huan], instructing the duke not to descend from his throne to bow. Duke Huan replied, "When the awe of heaven is but a few inches away, how could I, Xiaobai 小白, dare to sully the awesome command of the king?"[59] In the present, the Son of Heaven is of brilliant sagacity and his imperial spirit spreads far and wide, but it does not compare to the time of the King of Zhou. Your king consistently values ritual propriety and truly surpasses the sincerity of Duke Huan's reverence for civilization and veneration of the king. He could hardly

59 The devotion of the duke to the king was such that even when the king gave permission not to bow to the royal messenger, the duke did it anyway. This anecdote comes from the Zuo 左 commentaries to the *Spring and Autumn Annals*. See Feng Lihua and Lu Hao, eds., Zuo xiu, 5:12a; *Zuo Tradition, Volume One*, 292-3.

do more. The people sing his praises and the world rejoices in his beautiful deeds. In this it is possible to see how far the flourishing of the emperor's having unified the wheel gauges and scripts[60] has spread. We shall respectfully inform the throne and illumine his worthiness. The letter is attached.

April 17, 1537

(3/8)

Overcast.

It rained in the afternoon. The envoys left at seven o'clock in the morning and later arrived at Imjin 臨津. They summoned the reception envoy and the governor and they all sat together in the official yacht upon the river, drinking several rounds of wine while fishermen offered them a few carp. The envoys stood at the edge of the boat and, attaching lines to

60 The sovereign standardizes the wheel gauges of wagons so that the wagons and their ruts fit one another and people and goods may travel throughout the realm. Similarly, the sovereign unifies the many scripts into a single standard script so that people may easily communicate. This turn of phrase may be taken to encompass the moral influence of the sovereign as well. Such is the case where Gong Yongqing uses the phrase to indicate the Ming emperor's moral influence over Chosŏn, as indicated by the observance of ritual propriety. See "Zhongyong" in *Xinchu jingjiao sishu buzhu beizhi* ed. Deng Lin (Shanghai: Tianbao Shuju, 1916), 1:19a.

the fishes' mouths, they put them in the water to watch them swim around.

At one o'clock in the afternoon, the envoys arrived at P'aju 坡州 and had lunch. As the sun was setting in the west, they departed in the rain, later arriving at Pyŏkche-gwan 碧蹄館. First State Councilor (*yŏngŭijŏng* 領議政) Kim Kŭnsa 金謹思 and Minister of Rites (*yejo p'ansŏ* 禮曹判書) Yun In'gyŏng 尹仁鏡 had already arrived to serve as hosts. First Royal Secretary (*tosŭngji* 都承旨) Pak Hongnin 朴洪麟 served as special hospitality envoy. Third State Councilor (*uŭijŏng* 右議政) Yun Ŭnbo 尹殷輔 delivered the proclamation to the royal palace and then came [to P'yokche]. Once the welcoming ceremony for the proclamation was complete, the envoys each went to their quarters. Later, they came out and took their seats in the main hall. The first state councilor came in first, bowed, and then left. The third state councilor entered next and instructed Yi Hwajong to inform [the envoys] that he had delivered the proclamation to the royal palace. The envoys replied, "We have decided that tomorrow we will meet the high officials at Hongje-gwan 洪濟館 and then proceed to the royal palace and experience for ourselves the sincere heart of His Highness." Once the third state councilor left, the reception envoy and the governor saluted and left as well.

The chief envoy went to the assistant envoy's quarters where the two ate together before the welcoming banquet. Yi Hwajong reported to the envoys, "There are many officials who have already joined the banquet and the western wall of the hall is not very long, so they cannot all sit there. Thus I have dared to report."

The envoys replied, "Have the first state councilor sit on the eastern side on this occasion." The old precedent dictated that when the chief state councilor arrived at Pyŏkche-gwan to welcome the envoys, he was to sit on the west wall but this time the envoys permitted him to sit on the east side. This set a new precedent.

The first royal secretary went forward first and offered a cup of wine in welcome. Once the first state councilor and the minister of rites had each done the same, those ranking below the first state councilor followed. When the banquet was not yet finished, Fifth Royal Secretary (*ubusŭngji* 右副承旨) Hwang Ki 黃琦 arrived to request that the celestial envoys remain at Pyŏkche-gwan and delay their arrival in the capital until April 20 (3/11). When the banquet was over, Hwang reported to the envoys, "The king has sent me."

The envoys said, "You may speak now." Hwang Ki approached and bowed before instructing Yi Hwajong to report to the envoys, "With the rain situation as it is, if we welcome the proclamation tomorrow, we fear we may not be able to complete the ceremonies. His Majesty has especially dispatched one of his close officials to request that the two august gentlemen please wait two days and arrive in the capital on April 20 (3/11). Since the welcoming of a proclamation is an important matter, we calculated an auspicious day, and there were two conclusions: April 18 (3/9) and 20. Since we cannot welcome the proclamation on April 18, we dare to propose April 20."

The chief envoy and the assistant envoy lowered their heads in consultation for a considerable amount of time until finally they said, "We are quite displeased with delaying the reception of the proclamation and waiting here. Tomorrow we will go to Hongje-gwan or Mohwa-gwan 慕華館 and wait for the rain to clear before conducting the ceremonies. This will make it convenient for the king to attend to us."

Yi Hwajong answered directly, "Neither Hongje-gwan nor Mohwa-gwan have sleeping accommodations; they are just empty halls. It is not possible to stay in either place."

The envoys replied, "In that case, if the rain does not stop tomorrow, we will stay here as you have proposed. If the weather clears, we will depart for the capital. Go back and report to His Majesty that whether the rain clears or not will determine whether we go or not. Tomorrow morning, we will speak to Minister Chŏng[61] and have him relay our decision immediately."

The chief envoy's attendant was in the eastern chambers and delivered some poems the chief envoy had written. The interpreter Hong Kyŏm followed after him and was able to see the poems and memorize two of them. The first one read:

> Stream waters twist and turn beneath new willow color;
> A speeding carriage riles red dust the whole day through.
> Here at the edge of the world, what could be so urgent?
> Chirping swallows and soaring nightingales mock us to our deaths.

The second one read:

> Darkening mountain hues, day now turns to night;
> Deep within the dense forest: magpies' incessant chatter.
> Sea tides like this spring mountain rain;
> At the little landing, ripples fade into calm.

On this night, both of the state councilors and both of the royal

61 This is Chŏng Saryong, the reception envoy.

secretaries returned [to the capital].

April 18, 1537

(3/9)

Seemed like rain. Stayed at Pyŏkche-gwan.

The chief envoy arose from his bed at dawn. Yi Hwajong had a servant ask as to whether they would stay or leave. The chief envoy was furious and yelled at the servant, "The decision to stay or go resides with me! Why do you irritate with these questions? I want to to take some time to examine the rain situation and then decide. Why do you impertinently question me with what you have overheard?"

At breakfast, he sat outside his room. Yi Hwajong approached him and said, "Last night you issued the order to speak with Minister Chŏng and have him rely your decision immediately, so I have dared to ask about the decision to stay or to leave."

The chief envoy said, "It is forty *li* from here to the capital. If it looked like the rain was going to stop, why would I be sitting here? If we arrived at Hongje-gwan and changed into formal clothing, would your king be able to come?" Yi Hwajong replied to the effect that it would not be so easy to make such arrangements quickly. The chief envoy was angry and would not reply. The reception envoy quickly drafted a message and sent it to the Royal Secretariat.

At seven o'clock in the morning, the chief envoy, in casual clothing, went to the assistant envoy's quarters for consultation. The reception envoy wished to personally ask if they would stay or leave, so as he waited outside, he instructed an interpreter to tell the envoys. They emerged from their quarters, wearing their caps and belts, and took their seats in the main hall. The reception envoy approached them, saluted, and then said, "The proclamation, an expression of imperial grace, has almost arrived at capital and the king has mobilized his subjects and officials to welcome it with all due haste. The rain situation, however, has only gotten worse and will certainly not clear. His Majesty is concerned about waiting outside and is sincerely concerned that the integrity of the great ceremony will be marred."

The chief envoy replied, "We have brought the proclamation over ten-thousand *li* and now we must wait outside the capital. We are disappointed because previously we had decided to wait for the weather to clear and then enter the capital, but now, after having assessed the situation with the assistant envoy, it is clear that the rain will not break, making it likely that if the welcoming ceremonies are held, the situation would be chaotic. We have thus decided to stay here. Inform the king immediately."

The reception envoy asked, "How shall we proceed if the rain does not stop tomorrow?"

The chief envoy replied, "If that happens, we will discuss this again." The reception envoy then composed a message and sent it to the Royal Secretariat. Third Royal Secretary Hwang Hŏn 黃憲 came and inquired as to the well-being of the envoys and then requested that they enter the capital on April 20. Royal Logistics Officer (*sŏnjŏn'gwan* 宣傳官) Pak Ch'ŏlsu 朴鐵壽 arrived and said to Hwang Hŏn, "You must report to the celestial envoys the following, 'We are truly sorry that the envoys must stay in such crude accommodations. Naturally, the decision as to whether to stay or go rests with the august gentlemen.'"

Hwang Hŏn immediately transmitted these words to the envoys, who replied, "All official business for today is suspended and the day is already growing late; there is no time for new plans. Even if the rain does not stop tomorrow, we will go out into the rain and depart." The reception envoy composed a message and sent it to the Royal Secretariat. Third Royal

Secretary Kim Mi arrived and inquired as to the envoys' welfare. He also reported, "Today the king arrived at Mohwa-gwan and waited all day with the intention of hosting a banquet in the evening."

The reception envoy and the governor offered wine and then departed, following precedent.

April 19, 1537
(3/10)
Clear.

At dawn, the envoys took their seats in the main hall and ate together. They departed as soon they finished their meal. They arrived at the tent erected for them on the banks of the Tŏksu River (Tŏksu-ch'ŏn 德水川) where they briefly stopped for tea and cookies. At nine o'clock in the morning, they departed and later arrived at Hongje-wŏn. Minister of Rites Yun In'gyŏng and other officers on special assignment to attend to the embassy had already arrived and were waiting. The chief and assistant envoys conferred with one another and wrote up a list. Summoning the reception envoy, they said, "Yesterday we reviewed the ceremonial notes rather quickly, but now as we think about them, there are a number of elements that are not appropriate, so we have made this list to make the issues clear." They instructed the reception envoy to read it. When he had done so, they said, "You must urgently inform the king. If you do not follow this proper format in conducting the ceremonies, it would not be appropriate [for us] to participate in the banquet." The content was largely as follows:

> Guests and hosts should be seated to the south and north. Seating them to the east and west is really not proper etiquette. During the tea ceremony in the palace, after the bestowal of the proclamation and the imperial tablet is in place, seating guests facing north and hosts facing south is really rather awkward. In this case we must follow the ceremonial notes and seat the guests on the east and hosts on the west. In the case of meetings at T'aep'yŏng-gwan 太平館, T'aep'yŏng-gwan is our residence so we are the hosts and His Majesty is the guest. We should, however, defer to His Majesty so that he is seated on the north while we, conversely, are seated on the south. In the case of banquets, we are certainly the guests and we should face north and take the positon of guests. His Majesty is certainly the host so he should face south and take the position of host. If we conduct the ceremonies in this fashion, then both and guests and hosts will fulfil their ceremonial roles.

Such were the instructions. Assistant Section Chief of the Ministry of Rites (*yejo chwarang* 禮曹佐郞) Pak Chayŏng 朴自英 arrived and reported, "If we assign one or two people to take the proclamation to T'aep'yŏng-gwan, it would be no different than an ordinary interoffice document. We would prefer now to dispatch a specially-appointed officer with a ceremonial staff to accompany the proclamation to T'aep'yŏng-gwan."

The envoys said, "As this is not an [ordinary] edict, how could it be appropriate to employ such a protocol?" They then commanded their own attendants to manage the transport of the proclamation to T'aep'yŏng-gwan.

The reception envoy led the entire entourage to Mohwa-gwan where he first solemnly bowed [before the king] and then reported the two poems [by the chief envoy] that Hong Kyŏm had memorized. The king then spoke with him, asking whether he encountered any difficulties on the road. The envoys departed after lunch, passed through Sa-hyŏn 沙峴, presented the proclamation beneath Yŏngjo-mun 迎詔門,[62] and then took up their

---

62 Literally, the "Gate of Welcoming Proclamations." Originally there had only been a generic red balustrade gate, literally, a "red-arrow gate" (*hongjŏngmun* 紅箭門). As early as 1526, there had been some discussion in the Chosŏn court about replacing it with something grander. Indeed, when Ming envoys arrived in 1535, the existing gate was something of an embarrassment in its humbleness. In 1537, Kim Allo 金安老 and his colleagues on the State Council felt that the generic gate was insufficiently august for the purpose of welcoming Ming envoys and proposed building a larger four-pillared structure in the Ming style, but as no one knew in detail how to build such a gate, the Chosŏn government instead built a two-pillared gate with a blue tile roof entitled, *Yŏngjo-mun*, also recorded as *Yŏngjo chi mun* 迎詔之

positions on the left and right. The king then performed the five bows and three prostrations [before the proclamation] in a tent erected on the official road (*kwando* 官道) in front of Mohwa-gwan, after which he boarded his palanquin and returned to the palace first [before everyone else]. When the envoys were at Hongje-wŏn, they warned their attendants, "When his majesty is in the tent, you all must dismount and pass by on foot," so on this day, when the lead horsemen of the entourage passed the tent, they all dismounted and walked.

At one o'clock in the afternoon, the envoys entered the city walls and arrived at Kyŏngbok Palace (Kyŏngbok-gung 景福宮). The king commanded the the officials to perform the rites as indicated in the ceremonial notes. The king then changed clothes and ascended into the hall where tea was served, thereby completing the ceremony. The envoys then went to T'aep'yŏng-

---

門. In 1539, Ming envoy Xue Tingchong 薛廷寵 noted that the title of the still-new gate was too narrow as Ming envoys brought a variety of proclamations, edicts, and rewards from the Ming throne so he renamed it, "Gate of Welcoming Imperial Grace" (Yŏngŭn-mun 迎恩門). This gate was dismantled and replaced with the Independence Gate (Tongnim-mun 獨立門) in 1896-1898. Presently, only the stone footings of the pillars remain. See *Chungjong sillok* 21/6/13, 32/1/2; *Tongguk yŏji pigo* (Sŏul: Sŏul T'ŭkpyŏl-sisa P'yŏnch'an Wiwŏnhoe, 1956), 2:49; *Chŭngbo munhŏn pigo*, ed. Pak Yongdae et al., (Sŏul: Tongguk Munhwasa, 1959), 21:1a. Ŏ Sukkwŏn, "P'aegwan chapki," 141; Ŏ Sukkwŏn, *Storyteller's Miscellany*, 193-4. There are number of inconsistencies in the dating of these events across the sources. The *Tongguk yŏji pigo* 東國輿地備攷 suggests the new gate was built in 1535, but the *Chungjong sillok*, the more reliable source, indicates 1537. The *Tongguk yŏji pigo* also indicates that Ming envoy Xue Tingchong arrived in Chosŏn 1538, but in fact, he arrived in 1539. Ŏ Sukkwŏn's anecdote indicates that Xue arrived "three years after" 1537, but it was only two years later.

gwan to relax. The king later went to T'aep'yŏng-gwan to conduct the Dismounting Banquet (*hamayŏn* 下馬宴), which went on well into the night.

April 20, 1537

(3/11)

Clear.

The envoys stayed in T'aep'yŏng-gwan.

April 21, 1537

(3/12)

Clear.

The envoys stayed in T'aep'yŏng-gwan.

April 22, 1537

(3/13)

Clear.

The envoys stayed in T'aep'yŏng-gwan.

April 23, 1537

(3/14)

Clear.

The envoys stayed in T'aep'yŏng-gwan.

April 24, 1537

(3/15)

Clear.

The envoys stayed in T'aep'yŏng-gwan.

April 25, 1537

(3/16)

Clear.

The envoys stayed in T'aep'yŏng-gwan.

April 26, 1537

(3/17)

Rain.

The envoys were preparing to leave, but the rain did not stop. The king went to Mohwa-gwan and sent Sixth Royal Secretary *(tongbusŭngji* 同副承旨) Pak Suryang 朴守良 to ask the envoys to stay longer. The envoys replied, "Spring weather has always been rainy; how can it be avoided? The porters have already departed; it would not be appropriate for us to stay any longer." And so they stopped [asking], but the king sent Second Minister of Rites *(yejo ch'amp'an* 禮曹參判) Kim Kwangch'ŏl 金光轍 to ask again, but he did not even get the chance to speak. Then the king sent Third State Councilor Yun Ŭnbo to ask yet again.

The envoys replied, "We understand the generosity of His Majesty. Indeed, we already know, but the question has already been decided and it would not be appropriate to rescind it."

At nine o'clock in the morning, the envoys departed for Mohwa-gwan. The king had already prepared a banquet and was waiting for them. The envoys entered the hall and partook of the banquet, staying for quite a long time before leaving. The king walked to the front gate and again laid out cups of wine. They drank and then departed. When they arrived at Hongje-wŏn, they summoned the reception envoy and the capital host (*kwanban* 館伴) to sit together with them. They then composed some poetry, giving one poem to they capital reception envoy. Once they had completed the wine ceremony, they left, traveling through the night until they arrived at Pyŏkche-gwan. The king had already dispatched Second State Councilor (*chwaŭijŏng* 左議政) Kim Allo 金安老 and Minister of Rites Yun In'gyŏng to host a farewell dinner. He also specially dispatched First Royal Secretary Pak Hongnin 朴洪麟 to send off the envoys. The farewell banquet went deep into the night and on into the following morning.

The chief envoy instructed the interpreter to say to the reception envoy, "Previously I wrote a poem of regulated verse at this hall in appreciation of the king's concern for our well-being. Why have you mounted a different poem [on the wall] and not that one?"

The reception envoy replied, "If we had mounted that poem, people would misread it and fail to understand its connection with this hall, so we did not have it carved, [framed, and mounted]. Moreover, we sent the manuscript of the poem to the king as soon as you wrote it. Even if we wanted to have it carved and framed, we would not be able to remember it."

The chief envoy produced another copy and said, "My poem may be simple and blunt, but if you do not have my poem etched into a plaque and mounted here, how will future proclamation envoys know of what happened this day? Have this work done immediately and show it to me before our departure. Then you can have it mounted here later." The chief envoy also produced some miscellaneous poems he had previously written on the road and used a brush to make some annotations indicating which poem was to be mounted at which of the nearby stations and pavilions. The reception envoy immediately had the Pyŏkche-gwan poem carved into a plaque. He also copied the texts of those poems that had been excluded when the other plaques had been carved and sent them to each of the officials along the remaining route the envoys would take, and told them to have the plaques made and mounted by the time the envoys were to arrive.

April 27, 1537

(3/18)

Clear.

The reception envoy, second state councilor, and the minister of rites wrote poems in response to those written by the envoys when they were at T'aep'yŏng-gwan and as they were leaving Hansŏng 漢城.[63] These were bound and presented to the chief envoy, who replied, "These are all beautifully composed. Thank you so much, thank you!"

At seven o'clock in the morning, there was a farewell banquet in the main hall. The envoys came out and took their seats. The Second State Councilor sat to the east while the reception envoy, the minister of rites, the governor, and the first royal secretary sat together to the west. The first royal secretary offered the first cup of farewell wine. The second state councilor and the minister of rites then followed in succession. And each of the others below the second state councilor conducted the wine ceremony as well. Once this was complete, the envoys returned to their

63 This is a reference to Seoul.

quarters for a brief break. Soon the chief envoy came out again and stood, speaking with the second state councilor and the others, "When your country dispatches an envoy to express gratitude for imperial grace (*xieenshi* 謝恩使),[64] wait for about one month. Wait until the day we return to the capital, then the envoy can begin his journey."

The second state councilor composed a farewell poem and presented it to the envoys. They thanked him and praised his talent, "You are truly masterful!"

The chief envoy also said, "Although your country has a great deal of fine seafood, you still do not understand how to prepare it. This is a great shame so I will write out the methods and send them on to you." The chief envoy wrote a farewell poem at Mohwa-gwan and composed a letter, both of which he gave to the second state councilor, instructing him to present them to the king. The letter read as follows:

> Our meeting here at the very end of the earth was beyond all dreams and imagination. Having received the sincere hospitality of this worthy frontier domain, we have come to know deeply of its beautiful sentiments. And when the

64 This is the envoy the Chosŏn court would have to send to the Ming court to express gratitude for the proclamation of the birth of the crown prince.

officials came to Pyŏkche-gwan, the banquet was even more lavish. How could such a coarse person as myself be able to cope with it? It is ever more etched into my memory. I hope from afar that after our departure, your august person remains in fine health and your country receives great fortune.

The assistant envoy also presented a letter that read as follows:

> I was worried that Chosŏn would not hold in awe our imperial charge, but the service Chosŏn rendered made me ashamed to have harbored such concerns. While we stayed at T'aep'yŏng-gwan, the king personally visited several times, his attendants called upon us several times per day, and his letters expressing his sincere emotions arrived multiple times per day. And when we met, you seemed overwhelmed by humility. I know that all of these are instances of your respectful and abundant reverence for the imperial court. There are lines from the "The Hawfinches" that read, "Lead them to the left, lead them to the right, there are none who do not follow; lead them to right, lead them to the left, all do so correctly."[65]

65 Wu Ximeng, the assistant envoy, is citing the poem "Hawfinches" (Sanghu 桑扈) from the *Book of Odes*. The lines he paraphrases, however, are from a different poem, "Splendid are the Flowers" (*Changchang zhe hua* 裳裳者華), also from the *Book of Odes*. These lines describe lords in their chariots, leading their teams of horses flawlessly to the left and right, but we may read it as a metaphor for a sovereign and his lords or ministers, who are obedient and perform effortlessly and correctly in all circumstances. See "Sanghu" in *Shijing beizhi* ed. Zou Shengmai (Shanghai: Wensheng Shuju, 1904), 5:17a-18a.

This speaks to perfected talent. There is a line from "Distant Pouring" that reads, "The lord at peace is the mother and father of his people."[66] This speaks to enabling the people. In "Southern Mountains" there is the line, "Joyful gentlemen are the light of the country."[67] This speaks to completely fulfilling the duties of a subject, and even increasing their gravity. If the ministers to the left and right are of perfected talent and fully take responsibility for the people, then they will certainly become the light of the country.[68] Gazing east [toward Chosŏn], I will long remember Minister Kim's Pyŏkche-gwan banquet. In this way I respectfully express my gratitude and great happiness.

As the assistant envoy was about to depart, he pointed to an arrangement of paper birds and flowers and said, "I have elderly parents; I wish to take one of these back and show them."

At nine o'clock in the morning, the embassy departed at arrived at P'aju.

---

66 Wu here quotes another poem from the *Book of Odes*, "Distant Pouring" (*Jiongzhuo* 泂酌). The notion of a "distant pouring" in this instance suggests that the sovereign pours life-sustaining water that spreads to the far reaches of his realm. In this way he is a caring provider and parent to his people. See "Jiongzhuo" in *Shijing beizhi* ed. Zou Shengmai (Shanghai: Wensheng Shuju, 1904), 6:17a-17b.

67 In his third citation of the *Book of Odes*, Wu quotes the poem "Sedge of the Southern Mountains" (*Nanshan you tai* 南山有臺). We can understand "gentlemen" here to be those cultivated men who serve the state. They are joyful in their service and so constitute the light of the state. See "Nanshan you tai" in *Shijing beizhi* ed. Zou Shengmai (Shanghai: Wensheng Shuju, 1904), 4:8a-9a.

68 Wu is suggesting here that the king and his officials have perfectly fulfilled their duties in hosting the Ming mission.

During lunch, they went up into a small pavilion in front of the eastern chambers to look around. The chief envoy said, "Grandfather Wu wishes to name this pavilion "Drops of Blue" (C. *dicui*, K. *chŏkch'wi* 滴翠)."

The embassy departed at three o'clock in the afternoon and arrived at the Imjin River by the time the sun was beginning to set. The envoys went up into the pavilion at the riverside and examined the pavilion plaques for which they had written the texts. Soon thereafter they boarded an official yacht and called the reception envoy and the governor to sit together with them. And then they had wine poured. Fishermen caught several carp, but the envoys instructed them to run a line through the noses of the fish and release them back into the river. The envoys approached the river and watched the carp, laughing with delight. It was dark by the time the embassy reached Tongp'a-gwan. As it was already late in the evening, they ordered the banquet postponed until the following morning. The chief envoy instructed the interpreter to say to the reception envoy, "Has this place no oysters? Why can't you provide any? In the future you must arrange in advance for oysters at our accommodations."

April 28, 1537

(3/19)

Overcast.

The court commanded the presentation of the poems written by Minister Sim Ŏn'gwang 沈彥光 to the envoys. They read them over and said, "Excellent poems. Thank you very much."

At seven o'clock in the morning, the meal was ready in the main hall. The chief envoy said, "When we first came through here, you presented female entertainers. At that time, we accepted them because it was correct to be in accordance with the protocols of your country for hosting proclamation envoys. We also wished to respect the generosity of your king. Now, the mission has been completed and the sincerity of your country has been abundantly manifest. From now on, however, starting from Kaesŏng, do not present female entertainers again."

The envoys departed for Ch'ohyŏn-wŏn 招賢院. Upon arrival they took their seats in the tent there erected but said, "There are no buildings here; how can we stay here?" They went back into their palanquins and commanded an immediate departure.

The reception envoy said, "Kaesŏng is 26 or 27 *li* from here. The kitchen staff report that they have prepared tea and cookies and request that you allow them to approach the palanquins and present them to you."

The envoys said, "Such is the minister's desire to host his guests! Honestly, we cannot bear to refrain. We will partake and then depart quickly." And so, they had tea and cookies in their palanquins and then left.

At one o'clock in the afternoon, the envoys reached the offices of the Kaesŏng magistracy, whereupon they said to Yi Hwajong, "Fortunately, the sun has not yet set, so we wish to see the old sites of the city. Be sure not to allow the porters and to disperse while we are gone."

The host office replied, "The old sites are nothing but ruins now; there is nothing worth seeing. Moreover, the streets are too narrow for the embassy to pass. There has never been a case where proclamation envoys have toured the city."

The chief envoy replied angrily, "Just take us through the city! Why do you forbid it?"

And so, they dismissed the mounted escort and went ahead into the city in their palanquins. The reception envoy, the governor, and the Kaesŏng magistrate conferred and decided to send people ahead by a shortcut to Manwŏl-tae 滿月臺 to erect a tent. Soon thereafter, the envoys arrived with their attendants and interpreters. The group climbed a hill behind the site from which they could survey the whole area. There they stayed for quite some time before finally coming back down. The reception envoy offered them some wine but they refused. The chief envoy said to Yi Hwajong, "The palace foundations are quite large. Why are there no remains of the palace itself?"

Yi Hwajong replied, "Many years have passed so no part of it has survived."

Having quickly returned to the magistracy offices, the banquet began at three o'clock in the afternoon. Once the envoys took their seats, the farewell banquet hosts Hŏ Hŭp 許洽, and Hwang Ki, the reception envoy, the governor, and the Kaesŏng magistrate all greeted them and then took their seats on the west wall. As the banquet began, female entertainers filed in. The chief envoy said, "Yesterday, we told you not to provide female entertainers and the minister said he would obey our command, so why has he provided female entertainers today?"

The reception envoy replied, "Although we heard your command yesterday, we received no royal command forbidding the provision of female entertainers. Moreover, we did receive His Majesty's command to hold this farewell banquet. We did not dare to make changes to the arrangements on our own initiative."

The envoys relied, "If this is the case, we can accommodate your request temporarily." Secretary Hwang Hŏn first raised his cup in farewell and then the farewell banquet hosts, the reception envoy, and all the others also did so in turn.

When the embassy had first come across the Amnok River, the attendants Gao Song and Kang Zhen 康鎮 had presented a note to the reception envoy, saying, "This is the request of the Great Man of Liaodong."[69] The reception envoy, however, did not believe them and never transmitted the note to the [Chosŏn] court. Now as the embassy was on the return journey, they came to him and said, "He wishes to hear the reply."

---

69 The great man of Liaodong (C. *Liaodong daren*, K. *Yodong taein* 遼東大人) was the honorific term for the Liaodong Regional Military Commissioner (*Liaodong du zhihui shi* 遼東都指揮使) who served as the military governor of the Liaodong region.

April 29, 1537

(3/20)

Clear.

[The reception envoy] sent a message to the court asking how to respond, first, to the note from the Great Man of Liaodong that Gao Song and his associate had delivered[70] and, second, to the envoys' intention to visit T'onggun-jŏng 統軍亭 upon their arrival in Ŭiju.[71]

The envoys took their seats in the main hall and said to the farewell banquet hosts, "Previously His Majesty agreed to provide us with copies of the gazetteer (*chiji* 地誌) and roster of exam passers (*Tŭnggwa* 登科). Why haven't they arrived yet? Go back to His Majesty and tell him that we are waiting."[72] Both envoys wrote poems and gave them to the hosts. The chief envoy also produced a piece called, "Song of Kyŏnghoe Pavilion" (*Kyŏnghoe-ru ka* 慶會

70 It is not clear how this matter was resolved as it does not appear in the text again.

71 T'onggun Pavilion, was a sensitive military observation platform and, in times of war, a command post, that overlooked the Yalu River near Ŭiju. It is possible that for these reasons, the envoys' intention to inspect it raised some concern among the Chosŏn officials accompanying the embassy.

72 This was the source of some discord between the envoys and Chŏng Saryong. While not recorded here, Ŏ Sukkwŏn wrote that the Chosŏn failure to present these texts promptly gave some offense to Gong Yongqing. See Ŏ Sukkwŏn, "P'aegwan chapki," 142; Ŏ Sukkwŏn, *Storyteller's Miscellany*, 196.

樓歌) and gave it to the hosts to give to the king. The assistant envoy wrote out the text and characters for the new plaque for Chŏkch'wi-jŏng 滴翠亭 and gave them to the reception envoy, telling him, "You can give this to an officer at P'aju and tell him to have the plaque prepared and mounted."

At seven o'clock in the morning, the envoys departed for Sanye Post Station (Sanye-yŏk 狻猊驛). Upon their arrival, they sat down two *li* to the east of the station and had a tent erected at the side of the road. A person from Kaesŏng caught some fish and placed them in a fenced-off portion of the stream. The envoys approached and watched with delight, later fully releasing them back into the stream.

At ten o'clock in the morning, the embassy reached Kŭmgyo-gwan 金郊館, had lunch, and immediately departed for Ojo-ch'ŏn 吾助川. The envoys walked up and down the riverside enjoying the landscape for quite a while until they finally took their seats in the tent erected on the river bank. They called the reception envoy and the governor to sit with them for some wine. The chief envoy said, "Does anyone here play the flute?" The reply was, "No," so the chief envoy told the attendants to go up the cliff by the riverside and play the flute and pipe while the envoys and officers drank their wine.

The chief envoy said to the governor, "Have you had the plaque made yet for my 'Record of Ch'wibyŏng Mountain (*Ch'wibyŏngsan ki* 翠屛山記)?"'

The governor replied, "It has already been made and mounted."

The chief envoy said, "It is easy to have the text carved into wood but it would take a long time to have it carved into stone.

The governor conferred with the reception envoy and then replied, "This is an excellent idea, but it is not something that I can do on my own initiative. I must first report to His Majesty."

The chief envoy said, "When you erect the stele, make a rubbing of the text and send ten copies to us so we can see your sincerity. Also, when you print the next edition of the *Brilliant Flowers Anthology*, be sure to include the poems of the previous envoys. And do not be bound by precedent; send us many copies!"

The embassy traveled into the night before finally arriving at Hŭngŭi-gwan 興義館. The envoys postponed the banquet until the following morning.

April 30, 1537

(3/21)

Clear.

At seven o'clock in the morning, breakfast was prepared in the main hall. The envoys took their seats. The reception envoy and governor greeted them and then reported that a message from the king had arrived expressing his appreciation of the poems the envoys had written, along with a list of gifts. The envoys replied, "We have already not dared to accept the many gifts the king presented to us at Kyŏnghoe-ru and Kŭnjŏng-jŏn 勤政殿, but in the case of smaller individual gifts, we could not refuse them because we did not wish to reject the king's sincerity. Even so, we were not comfortable in doing so, and now as the gifts arrive here on the road, our minds are not any more at ease. How can we possibly accept them?"

The reception envoy tried two or three times to convince the envoys to accept the gifts, but the envoys said, "Such is the sincerity of the king, if we now too strictly reject these gifts, we fear that we might cause some inconvenience." Each envoy then accepted five bolts each of white ramie cloth and black hempen cloth, saying, "We accept these only to acknowledge the sincerity of the king, nothing more." Once they accepted the cloth, the interpreter Yi Yŏngjŏng 李永貞 left, and the envoys had a meal of rice and soup.

The reception envoy instructed Yi Hwajong to give the gifts they had brought from the capital to Gao Song and the other attendants, and to explain that the Ministry of Rites had printed the envoys' poetry. Gao Song replied, "It is difficult for us to take all of this now. Please send it along with the next envoy to express gratitude for imperial grace."

At nine o'clock in the morning, the envoys departed for Chŏt'an. Once they arrived they took their seats on the official yacht and called on the reception envoy and the governor to play *t'uho* with them. Then they instructed the two of them to play together. After the games were done, they had some wine and then finished.

They arrived at Posan-gwan 寶山館 in the evening and had dinner in the main hall. The envoys took their seats. The reception envoy and the governor entered, saluted them, and presented an abridged list of exam passers (*hoesi sorok* 會試小錄). The envoys read the list and said, "Excellent, excellent!" They said to the reception envoy, "We did not personally copy the poetry manuscripts we sent previously. The people who did copy them often wrote the wrong character or omitted some characters altogether, so we want to correct the manuscripts. Send them all back to us." They also said, "As we have a banquet every night, both guests and hosts have grown weary. We wish to cancel this evening's banquet." They then saluted and went to their quarters. That night, the chief envoy corrected several booklets of his poetry and then immediately sent them to the reception envoy.

May 1, 1537

(3/22)

Clear.

At nine o'clock in the morning the envoys departed for Ch'ongsu-san. When they arrived, they first went to the stele site and looked around. Then they went down to the bank of the stream where they crossed over a temporary bridge and sat beneath the bluff. Relaxing and enjoying themselves, they invited the reception envoy and governor to share some wine and join them in a guessing game for fun. The chief envoy issued a challenge, "If my guess is wrong, then the minister and I will have to drink.

If Mr. Wu[73] is wrong, then he and the governor will have to drink." As the two of them guessed correctly and incorrectly, everyone drank five or six cups of wine before the game was over. The envoys called for more wine and then engaged in some archery. The assistant envoy shot fifty or sixty arrows, but not one of them hit the target. They had the reception envoy and the governor shoot as well. After they had finished, the chief envoy had a tent erected beneath Ch'wibyŏng-san, the hill that he had named himself.

At one o'clock in the afternoon, the envoys went to the tent and called the reception envoy and the governor to sit with them, facing the hill. They instructed Ch'a Yunsŏng 車允成 to tell the governor, "If you were to build a pavilion here, it could really enhance the character of the landscape." And then he joked, "When the crown prince receives his investiture, we really should be the envoys again so we can come back to this mountain."

The assistant envoy raised his cup and asked of his companions, "This is the Ch'wibyŏng-san wine of the Scholar Yungang 雲岡![74] Leave not one drop behind!"

They eventually departed, arriving later at Ansŏng-gwan, where they

---

73 This is the assistant envoy, Wu Ximeng.
74 "Yungang" is the pen name of the chief envoy.

had lunch. They then traveled on into the night before finally arriving at Yongch'ŏn-gwan. The envoys postponed the banquet until the following morning.

May 2, 1537
(3/23)
Clear.

At seven o'clock in the morning, the envoys took their seats in a tent erected on a hill in front of Yongch'ŏn-gwan, whereupon the banquet table was presented. The assistant envoy shot some arrows at a target and then had the reception envoy and the governor do the same. There were offerings of wine before the banquet ended. The envoys then departed for Kŏmsu-gwan where they had lunch and then again departed, later arriving in Pongsan. The envoys walked to Sŏbong-jŏng 棲鳳亭 and examined the plaque. The chief envoy said, "The characters seem to have lost much of their original form [as they were carved for the plaque] and the title seems lopsided. It really is not much to look at." He commanded that the plaque be taken down and then used some black ink to correct the calligraphy. He gave the result to the reception envoy and told him to have the plaque redone accordingly.

The reception envoy instructed Hong Kyŏm to say to the chief envoy, "When we were coming here we were quite busy so I delegated the task to the Commission[75] but I did not know that the original form of the characters was so deformed during the carving process. I am absolutely mortified. Even though you have now corrected the calligraphy, I fear it is not as it originally was. It seems that the text was copied poorly. I will instruct the governor to have the plaque redone by a master craftsman."

The chief envoy replied, "I will rewrite it and send it later."

Ever since the envoys had departed Seoul, whenever they arrived at a guest house or post station, the examined the plaques of the calligraphy they themselves had written, and if there was a single stroke that did not meet with their approval, they commanded that the plaque be taken down so they could correct it. And when they presented a poem they recited on the road with no relation to a particular guest house or post station, they would ask the reception envoy, "Why is this the only poem you have not

75 This is the Reception Commission (*wŏnjŏp togam* 遠接都監), an *ad hoc* Chosŏn agency established to manage the hosting of the Ming envoys.

had carved into a plaque and mounted? Have the plaque made tonight and show us the finished product in the morning!" The reception envoy had no choice but to copy all the poems the envoys had written for each place they had been and send them ahead to each stop on the itinerary so that the plaques could be made and mounted before the envoys' arrival.

In the evening, the banquet was in the main hall. The envoys said to the reception envoy, "Although the abridged record of the *hoesi* that the king sent yesterday was nice, it was frequently rather vague. We want to know about the format and rules for the roster of exam passers. We do not need to see the rosters for many exams; just one or two will do. We would like to see which person passed with highest grade in what year, how many people passed which exams in a given year. How old were they, from where did they come, and who were their parents? Record this information and send it to us. It would be a shame if we came all the way here and witnessed the abundance of your cultural achievements but did not learn about your examination system. Quickly tell the king to record this information and show us."

The reception envoy replied, "In this country we do not record the age of the examinees on roster of exam passers."

The envoys said, "If that is the case, then show us the roster as it is presently formatted." They also said, "In the matter of the provision of female entertainers, we already know of the king's sincerity in hosting his guests. We request that during the banquet in Hwangju tomorrow, you do not provide them."

The reception envoy replied, "The farewell banquet host has received His Majesty's command to host you; he cannot act on his own initiative [to forego the female entertainers]. We will have to discuss the matter."

The assistant envoy sent several poems, including one entitled, "Remembering Qin E" (*Yi Qin e* 憶秦娥), words to the [well-known] song. As the rhyme scheme seemed different, the reception envoy did not write a poem in response. The assistant envoy demanded an immediate response. The reception envoy replied, "The sounds of the languages of this country and the Central State are quite different. The differences are even more pronounced in poem and song. Even if you were to force me to write a poem in reply, it would not go well. Years ago when Director Qi Shun 祈順[76] came here, he composed the lyrics to ten songs, and one of the hosts, Minister Sŏ Kŏjŏng 徐居正, wrote a poem in response to each one, but he was only able to keep the rhyme but not the proper stressed syllables. One

76 Qi Shun was a Ming envoy who came to Chosŏn in 1476 to announce the investiture of the Ming crown prince.

cannot avoid the differences in stressed syllables so I now do not dare to write a poem in response."[77]

May 3, 1537

(3/24)

Overcast.

At seven o'clock in the morning, the envoys took their seats in the main hall. The reception envoy and the governor entered the hall and saluted the envoys. The envoys said, "We wish to see the civil service examination rosters for both of you. Prepare them quickly and show them to us." The assistant envoy produced the text he had written for the plaque for Yosan-jŏng 樂山亭 and gave it [to us]. The envoys walked to the Sŏbong-jŏng and looked out over the landscape. Then they walked around the steps to the reception envoy's quarters for a time to look at the red peonies.

The envoys then departed for Sari-wŏn where they had a brief lunch

77 See Ŏ Sukkwŏn, "Paegwan chapki," 132; Ŏ Sukkwŏn, *Storyteller's Miscellany*, 152-3.

before again departing for Kŭksŏng 棘城 where they had tea. They went up to the top of a hill by the side of the road to look at the sea. Pointing to Kuwŏl Mountain (Kuwŏl-san 九月山), they asked, "What is the name of that mountain?" The interpreter replied factually.

At three o'clock in the afternoon, they arrived at Chugŭm-gye 簇錦溪 in Hwangju where they boarded an official yacht. When the envoys saw the plaques of their poetry, they were absolutely delighted and called for some wine. They asked the P'yŏngsan Magistrate Yi Rim, "When did you pass the civil service examination?"

"I passed in 1524," he replied.

The chief envoy asked, "The examinations are held once every three years and 1524 does not fall within that schedule so how is that you say you passed in 1524?"

The magistrate explained, "In this country, there are examinations held outside this schedule, called 'special examinations,' from which candidates for office are selected." The chief envoy asked when the magistrate was born and he replied, "I was born in 1501."[78]

The chief envoy said, "One might say that you were rather young to

78 Yi Rim's literal reply was, "The *sinyu* 辛酉 year of the Hongch'i (C. Hongzhi 弘治) Reign." Yi was careful to use the Ming reign period on the company of the Ming envoys.

pass the examination. I want to see the roster. When we get to the offices in Hwangju, copy it and show me."

The envoys noted that the reception envoy and the governor had neither fish nor meat on their plates and asked why. They replied, "Today we refrain in memory of our deceased queen."

In the evening when they arrived at the guest house in Hwangju, the envoys postponed the banquet until the following day and then went to Kwangwŏl-lu 廣遠樓 and played *t'uho*. The assistant envoy shot a few archery rounds and invited the reception envoy and the governor to join him, but they replied, "Today is the memorial day for the deceased queen. Please invite us again tomorrow."

The chief envoy said, "His Majesty has dispatched you and your staff to this place to host us. Why must you uphold this memorial observance and mar our welcome today?"

In the evening, the chief envoy said to the reception envoy, "I want to read about the founding of the state in this eastern land, and about the royal genealogy and historical chronology. Write them and show me."

May 4, 1537

(3/25)

Overcast.

The interpreter provided the envoys with the civil service examination rosters of the reception envoy, the governor, and the P'yŏngsan magistrate, as well as an abridged account of the founding of the state and a historical chronology. The chief envoy wrote a short note to the reception envoy that read, "How many examinees are selected from each of the provincial examinations? Who oversees the examinations? Where are they sent and how many are there? Write the answers to these questions in detail and give them to me."

The reception envoy had the following written and given to the chief envoy: "Three hundred are chosen from the provincial examinations across the whole of the eight provinces. When the provincial governors are going to hold examinations, they report to the court, which in turn, dispatches civil officials from the capital to serve as examiners, four to each province."

At seven o'clock in the morning, the farewell banquet was prepared in Kwangwŏl-lu. The envoys took their seats. The reception envoy, the governor, and the banquet host Kim Kwangch'ŏl entered and greeted the envoys. They presented the gazetteer that had been sent from the capital the previous day, as well as the reciprocal poems from banquet host in Kaesŏng. [We] also informed the envoys that many officials who had been involved in hosting the embassy had received promotions, that there would be special examinations in honor of the proclamation, and that the king was giving a banquet on the occasion of the birth of the imperial crown prince. Upon hearing this, the envoys turned to one another in delight, and replied, "The birth of the imperial crown prince is an Occasion of Great Joy for all the world in equal measure! The arrival of this proclamation is an act of remarkable imperial grace. Your country has always taken ritual propriety seriously, and this is to celebrated, but to have spread the imperial grace so broadly among the subjects could only be possible by virtue of the worthiness of His Majesty! Upon our return we will submit a memorial to inform the court of this." They also said, "The gazetteer is quite detailed. Thank you so much. We will take pleasure in it for years to come. And thank you for all the beautiful poems you have given us."

They envoys also said to the reception envoy, "Starting from today, do not provide any female entertainers."

The reception envoy replied, "His Majesty dispatched the banquet host to this place to host you. All that we do emerges from his will. If we do not provide female entertainers, what will the say when he reports to the throne?"

The envoys replied, "Respect is not to be expressed through entertainment. Heeding our words today and not providing female entertainers – *that* is respect."

The banquet host stood before the envoys and pleaded with them to allow the female entertainers. The envoys conferred with one another at length until finally they said, "Now, for the sake of the minister and others, we will have a performance with the instruments we have brought with us and then we will accommodate the provision of female entertainers." And so they instructed two attendants to take up the instruments and play. One person donned a mask and performed playfully. In all, four or five people performed in this way. When they were finished, the female entertainers from our country performed before the envoys, thereby concluding the banquet.

After the banquet, the envoys practiced some archery at Kwangwŏl-lu. They invited the reception envoy and the governor to join them, having them shoot several rounds as well. The chief envoy rewrote the characters for the Sŏbong-jŏng plaque and the assistant envoy wrote the characters for the Chean-gwan 齊安館 plaque. They gave the texts to the governor and told him to have the plaques carved and mounted. The chief envoy wrote a poem and gave it to the banquet host. He also wrote two letters and gave them to the banquet host to give to the king. The assistant envoy wrote a poem and gave it to the banquet host to give to the king. He also wrote a letter and instructed that it should be given to the king.

At one o'clock in the afternoon, the envoys departed for Chŏbog-wŏn where they had lunch. In the evening, they arrived at Saengyang-gwan. The envoys postponed the banquet until the following day. A runner from Ŭiju brought two official documents sent from Tang-zhan 湯站, which [we] immediately delivered to the envoys.

May 5, 1537

(3/26)

Clear.

The envoys each had a member of their households send a bolt of silken fabric to the reception envoy, saying, "We know well that these gifts are not especially impressive, but please accept them merely as tokens of our esteem." The chief envoy was seeking to acquire a sea otter pelt and two ink stones and said, "The Elder of the Hall[79] is looking for these items: a larger and a smaller ink stone, each intricately carved, and a sea otter pelt. You can trade some of the supplies we have brought with us to acquire these items."

The envoys took their seats in the main hall and had their morning meal. After the reception envoy saluted them, he expressed his gratitude, "I have hosted you for many days and during that time there have been many mistakes for which am constantly fearful. And now, you have bestowed these items, I am even more fearful. Moreover, I am uneasy in wondering if it is acceptable for me to personally receive such fabulous gifts."

The envoys replied, "The gifts are not good quality and we do not like them so do not thank us to strenuously."

The reception envoy then said, "I will look for the ink stones you seek along the way through P'yŏngan Province and bring them to you. The sea otter pelt, however, is not something produced in this country. There is no way to acquire one, and even if they were produced here, what would [we

---

79 This is a reference to the Ming Grand Secretary Li Shi.

appropriately] trade for it?"

The envoys passed by Chaesong-jŏng 栽松亭 and went directly to the Taedong River. The reception envoy and the governor boarded the official yacht and had some wine set out. Going upstream, they went to Pubyŏng-nu 浮碧樓 and had tea. The assistant envoy said, "The landscape here is even better than Paeksang-nu."

The chief envoy said, "At Paeksang-nu, all four directions are open and unimpeded. Here, one side rests upon the mountain. If we consider these sites from a geomantic perspective, then Pubyŏng-nu, with its back to the mountain while facing the water, is best. If we consider the quality of the vistas, then Paeksang-nu, with its uninterrupted views in all four directions, is best.

The governor had a troupe of entertainers put on a performance in the courtyard. The envoys sat and watched. Once the performance was over, the envoys boarded their palanquins and ascended to Moran Peak (Moran-bong 牡丹峯). Moran Peak is at the top of Kŭmsu Mountain (Kŭmsu-san 錦繡山). It is not an especially lofty mountain, but from the top the views are extensive. A ring of steep mountain peaks embraces everything near and far, binding all together in a great mass. At that time, many dark clouds had gathered and a light rain cleansed our faces. After a few minutes, however, the clouds broke and the envoys had some wine beneath a canopy. Then they went back down to Pubyŏng-nu for the banquet. There were female entertainers, but the envoys commanded that their own performers play amongst them. They arrived at Taedong-gwan in the early evening.

May 6, 1537
(3/27)
Clear.

It rained in the afternoon and the envoys remained in P'yŏngyang. The chief envoy sent an official document to Tianshui-zhan 甜水站. At seven o'clock in the morning, there was a banquet in the main hall. The envoys took their seats. The reception envoy, the governor, and the banquet host Hŏ Hang 許沆 entered the hall and greeted the envoys before taking their own seats. Female entertainers were in attendance as the banquet host was the first to raise his cup. The reception envoy and the others all did the same, in turn. When the banquet was over, the host approached the envoys and to tell them he was taking his leave. The envoys commanded Yi

Hwajong to say, "The king has sent the second minister[80] exclusively for us. Today we are staying here so we wish to tour the ancient sites. Surely the king knows this. It would be most fortunate if the second minister were to tour with us." And then they turned to the reception envoy and said, "Make the second minister stay!"

After the morning meal was over, the envoys went to the Tomb of Kija where they made offerings of incense and bowed. Then they went on past the remains of the well-fields[81] and arrived at the Yŏnggwi-ru 詠歸樓. When they were about to begin the banquet, a message arrived from the king that read to the effect of, "The two copies of the painting '*Welcoming the Proclamation*' that the celestial envoys wanted are complete and I send them now." The envoys looked at the paintings and were very happy. Ordering the seals opened, the pointed out various elements of the

---

80 The banquet host Hŏ Hang was the second minister of personnel (*ijo ch'amp'an* 吏曹參判).

81 The sage Kija (C. Jizi 箕子) was said to have come to Chosŏn from the state of Yin 殷 and implemented, among many other policies, the well-field system in which the state divided agricultural land into square parcels, each divided into nine smaller square plots of equal size. The state then allotted the outer eight plots to peasant households for their own use. The remaining central plot was to be cultivated cooperatively by the eight households who would submit the resulting harvest from the central plot to the state as their tax payment. This pattern of nine square plots looks like the character 井, meaning a "well" from which one would draw water. This form of land tenure has thus come to be known was the well-field system. For more on the notion of Kija having come to the P'yŏngyang area and implemented the well-field system, see Kang Boseong, "Land Reform in the Realization of a Confucian Ideal: The Debate among Neo-Confucian Scholars in the Mid-Chosŏn Period," *Acta Koreana* 25, no. 2 (December 2022): 1-18.

paintings to one another for quite a while. Expressing their happiness, they said, "Such is the king's consideration for us! We cannot thank him enough. These paintings will be our eternal family heirlooms."

The envoys moved the tables aside and sat together comfortably to east wall while the reception envoy and the others sat across from them to the west. They all spoke together quietly. The chief envoy said, "It seems that [our] court treats your country no differently than the inner domains. Indeed, Elder of the Hall Xia 夏[82] is increasingly supportive [of this approach]. He said about our mission, 'Even though you will travel thousands of miles, that place is a country of propriety and righteousness; their hospitality will ease a traveler's weariness.' He also wrote a poem and gave it to me, but I accidentally left it in Liaodong. When Grandfather Xia became an elder of the hall, it was indeed a lofty appointment." The chief envoy continued, "Elder of the Hall Xia's prose and calligraphy are the most beautifully refined among the high ministers at court. His calligraphy is widely praised as comparable to that of Zhang Donghai 張東海.[83] If the king were to submit a memorial requesting a sample of his calligraphy,

---

82 This is a reference to the Ming official Xia Yan 夏言 who had recently been promoted from the post of minister of rites to grand secretary, here colloquially rendered "elder of the hall" (*gelao* 閣老).

83 This is the famed Ming calligrapher Zhang Bi 張弼 (1425-1487). "Donghai" is his pen name.

the court would surely bestow the honor on the esteemed gentleman Xia and happily permit it. Elder of the Hall Xia, for his part, would surely be pleased to do it."

The reception envoy replied, "His Majesty respects and fears the [Ming] court. How could he dare to impose upon the Sagely Majesty to grant such a request?"

The envoys replied, "It would not be a problem."

The reception envoy then addressed the envoys, "For generations this country has enjoyed the favor of the Sagely Court (*sŏngjo* 聖朝)[84] as it has permitted [our] tributary envoys to leave [the official guesthouse in the Ming capital] freely and allowed them to procure books both old and new. Recently, however, Director of the Bureau of Receptions, Sun Cun 孫存, on his own initiative, ordered Bureau Secretary Wu Yu 仵瑜 to issue restrictions on Chosŏn people, refusing to permit them to leave [the guesthouse] as well as preventing them from buying books, be they official editions (*kwanbon* 官本) or historical chronicles. His Majesty has already sent a communication to the Board of Rites last year requesting freedom of movement [for Chosŏn officials] as in times past. Minister Xia[85] [forwarded

84 This a reference to the Ming court.
85 This refers to Xia Yan when he was the minister of rites prior to his promotion to grand

the request] in a memorial to the throne and the request was granted; [our] small country (*sobang* 小邦) was overcome with emotion and yet it appears as though official editions and historical chronicles remain prohibited. When I delivered a royal communication [to the Ming Board of Rites] in 1534,[86] the book sets we encountered were missing volumes and ultimately we were unable to purchase any official editions. Have these restrictions come from the [Ming] court?"[87]

The envoys replied in shock, "What are you talking about? The court favors your country more than any other. Indeed, the high officials have all taken it upon themselves, by the will of the emperor, to treat your country well. How could there be something like this? Even though we deem Annam and Liuqiu 琉球 barbarous, we still allow their children to come and study, so how could [officials from] your country, which is just like the inner zones of submission,[88] be prevented from leaving the guesthouse? If Director Sun has taken it upon himself to act in this way, then he is

---

secretary.

86 Chŏng Saryong was the Chosŏn winter solstice envoy (*tongjisa* 冬至使) to the Ming court in 1534. See Yi Hŭisŭng et al., comp., *Han'guk inmyŏng tae sajŏn* (Sŏul: Sin'gu Munhwasa, 1967), 828.

87 For further details on the dispute over the freedom of movement of Chosŏn envoys in Beijing, see *Chungjong Sillok* 17/2/3; Ŏ Sukkwŏn, "P'aegwan chapki," 118; Ŏ Sukkwŏn, *Storyteller's Miscellany*, 74-76.

88 This is a reference to the territory of the Ming Empire.

not fit for office and will be sent out to serve as a prefect [at some remote post]. Director of the Bureau of Ceremonies Chen Chi 陳箎 is a friend of ours. When we [were going to] come here, the esteemed gentleman Chen organized a banquet for us at which he said, 'Chosŏn is a country that takes ritual propriety seriously; you must not treat them lightly.' This shows his deep appreciation of Chosŏn. When we return to court, we will speak with the esteemed gentleman Chen and tell him not to enact these restrictions. He is a prudent, decent man and most certainly will not enforce Director Sun's rule." They also said, two or three times, "We will not forget this matter."

The reception envoy also asked, "When people in the past referred to those who came before, there were many examples of names like 'Han Eighteen' (Han Sip'al 韓十八) or 'Hwang Nine' (Hwang Ku 黃九). What did this mean? Did it refer to their official rank or perhaps their birth order among their siblings?"[89]

The chief envoy replied, "I will write this down in detail and show you [later]."

The reception envoy further asked, "Poets often use the two characters

---

89 On these sorts of conversations between Gong and Chŏng, see Ŏ Sukkwŏn, "P'aegwan chapki," 149; Ŏ Sukkwŏn, *Storyteller's Miscellany*, 237.

mun'gŏn 悶徤. What does this mean?"

The chief envoy explained, "This was from a regional dialect of the Tang 唐 and Song 宋 periods, similar to words like *zhemo* 遮莫 in the poetry of Du Fu 杜甫 (712-770), but this one means 'strong.'"

Again, the reception envoy asked, "And are there any remnants of the Eight Fortifications (*p'alchinjŏk* 八陣磧)?"[90]

The chief envoy replied, "There are a few places in Sichuan 四川 and Shanxi 陜西 where they are quite clear."

The reception envoy asked once more, "What are the pong fields (K. *pongjŏn*, C. *fengtian* 葑田) in Suzhou 蘇州 and Hangzhou 杭州?"

The envoys replied, "'*Feng*' 葑 (K. *pong*) is a plant that grows on the surface of the water and can be eaten when it first spouts. The roots are intertwined together and it floats on the surface of the water without any contact with the soil. They grow across wide areas reaching hundreds of *li* The local people call these enormous patches '*feng*' fields."

At that time, rain appeared on the river, sometimes in single distant drops, sometimes in a fine spray. As evening approached, the rain stopped

---

90 This term refers to the creative defensive installations that Zhuge Liang 諸葛亮 (181-234) of the state of Shu Han 蜀漢 built, largely to disorient the enemy and render them vulnerable to attack. See Sim Paekchun and Tam Ryangso, *Samguk chi sajŏn*, trans. Chŏng Wŏn'gi (Sŏul: Pŏmusa, 2000), 590.

and a long rainbow stretched across the sky. Its reflection appeared in the river water as the light of the setting sun shone through the clouds. A red hue filled the sky as the limitless heavens and waters all blended into a single color. The envoys leaned on the railing, craning to look, seemingly unable to bear the thought of getting up to leave. In the evening they returned to their guesthouse.

The chief envoy wrote a list of the people with whom the envoys had enjoyed themselves at Pubyŏng-nu which he sent to the reception envoy and the governor, instructing them to have the text carved into a boulder. The text read, "In April of 1537, Chief Envoy Gong Yongqing, Assistant Envoy Wu Ximeng, Minister Chŏng Saryong, and Governor Yi Kwiryŏng toured this area." At the end he also wrote, "Qing wrote this"[91] in characters as large as one's hand. The assistant envoy, too, wrote, "Pure Stream Bluff" (*Qing liu bi* 清流壁) in large characters and at the end added, "Meng wrote this."[92] They sent these too to the reception envoy, instructing him to have the texts carved into a boulder on the roadside near Pubyŏng-nu. The chief envoy directing him, "Have this carved deeply into stone

91 "Qing" is an abbreviation of the chief envoy's given name, Yongqing.
92 "Meng" here is an abbreviation of the assistant envoy's given name, Ximeng.

and filled with red pigment."[93] The chief envoy additionally wrote "River and sky, outstanding scenery" (*jiang tian sheng gai* 江天勝槪) and instructed that it should be carved into a plaque and mounted at Pubyŏng-nu.

Earlier when the chief envoy arrived at Kŭmgyo-gwan, he saw a plaque text the reception envoy had written and asked if the reception envoy had written it himself. He praised the calligraphy, "With a hand like this, why have someone else copy the poem [for the plaque]?" When they arrived in P'yŏngyang, he had the plaque of the poem he had written at K'waejae-jŏng 快哉亭 taken down to be corrected because it had overlapping characters. He had the reception envoy rewrite the text so it could be carved into a new plaque. He also instructed that several rubbings of the plaque be made and given to his attendant for safe keeping.

93 See Ŏ Sukkwŏn, "P'aegwan chapki," 151; Ŏ Sukkwŏn, *Storyteller's Miscellany*, 245.

May 7, 1537

(3/28)

Sometimes clear, sometimes overcast.

At seven o'clock in the morning, the envoys emerged [from their quarters] and took their seats in the main hall. The reception envoy and the others entered and greeted the envoys. The hospitality envoy stepped forward and reported that he would take his leave. The envoys each gave him a farewell poem and a letter to deliver to the king. The letter from the chief envoy read:

> I have received the painting *Welcoming the Proclamation.* The colors strike the eye like a treasured jewel. Feeling your sincere generosity from afar, how can I possibly thank you enough? When I opened it fully and looked at its contents, I could see all the mountains, rivers, and indeed, the very culture of the country. This painting will be viewed generation after generation and is a treasure truly worthy of being passed down in our family. Unable to fully express my feelings, how could I dare to speak of them? When Second Minister Hŏ returns and reports to the throne, he will express my sincere gratitude and shining happiness.

The letter from the assistant envoy read:

> When we arrived in Hwangju, I was thankful for the king having sent his representatives to prepare a banquet for us. And when we arrived at Saengyang-gwan 生陽館, still some one-hundred *li* away from P'yŏngyang, we were again grateful for the king having sent Second Minister of Personnel Hŏ to host a banquet for us. As a descendent from a long line of talented men, the second minister conducted himself properly in every respect. The reception envoy Minister Chŏng always treated us with an etiquette most proper and an elegance that only increased with time. Governor Yi provided the most marvelous entertainment and with the utmost sincerity showed us landscapes of beauty and wonder. He and Minister Chŏng together well expressed the sentiments of the king throughout our time here. We could see this throughout each day, causing us to admire the excellence the king, ministers, and all the people, high and low, of the Eastern State and to increase our respect one-thousand fold. Minister Chŏng has requested to accompany us to the lake west of Yŏnggwi-ru tomorrow, after we pay our respects at the Tomb of Kija. When I heard that the king had sent the painting *Welcoming the Proclamation*, I could hardly keep from jumping for joy! As I unrolled the scroll, I could see that every detail, great and small, had been included. The five bows outside the walls of the capital and the many officers attending to their duties – this has not happened in a long time and can only be seen once in a hundred years. And then

to receive this painting in addition – it is a demonstration of the king's respect for the emperor and the sincerity of his serving the great (C. *shida*, K. *sadae* 事大). The excellence of the men of the Eastern State, the superlative beauty of its mountains and rivers, the brilliance of its ceremony – all are shown together [in a single scene]. How could a coarse man such as myself have had the good fortune of being included in this painting? In the future when I am retired and sitting at home by myself, I will look on the scene in this painting and as my memories come flooding back, I will never tire of gazing into the east [toward Chosŏn]. When Second Minister Hŏ returns [to report to the throne], I can only hope that he is able to deliver some rough approximation of my gratitude.

The envoys then departed, later arriving at Pusan-wŏn where they invited the reception envoy and the governor to join them for some wine. They next arrived at Sunan 順安 and had lunch. One of the chamber servants (*pangsuin* 房守人) had been carrying the case for the ink stone from the capital that the assistant envoy had been using. The attendant Qian Xun 錢循 wanted to take it, but the servant refused to surrender it. [Qian Xun] tried to take it by force and, in the resulting scuffle, it fell to the ground and broke irreparably. The reception envoy heard about this and had another case made.

During the afternoon, the envoys passed through Ŏp'a Pass (Ŏp'a-ryŏng

於波嶺). Officers from Anju and elsewhere had erected a tent on a high hill to the west of the road and wanted to offer tea and cookies to the envoys, but they refused.[94] In the evening, the envoys arrived at Sukch'ŏn, where they postponed the banquet until the following morning. The chief envoy sat in the office during the night where he wrote poetry by candlelight. The office slave Kwŏn Son 權孫 went to the office two or three times to take away the burned candles. The chief envoy yelled at him to stop, but he would not listen. The chief envoy became angry, grabbed him, and sent him to the reception envoy and the governor, telling them to imprison [Kwŏn].

May 8, 1537

(3/29)

Clear.

The reception envoy and the governor sat together while they had Kwŏn Son beaten with a staff eighty times. They sent Yi Hwajong to

94 For an alternate translation of these two sentences, see Chŏng, *Chŏnsa illo ilgi*, 114.

report to the chief envoy, "The person who tried to take your candles last night was completely inappropriate. Now we have interrogated and sentenced him to labor at a distant post station on the frontier. We will report to His Majesty as soon as the punishment has been executed."

The chief envoy said, "The punishment has already been severe enough. Do not bother reporting it."

At seven o'clock in the morning, the banquet was held in the main hall. The attendant to the assistant envoy said, "This morning, Grandfather[95] took out the ink stone in the luggage, did some writing, and then left the ink stone on the desk without putting it away. There was a chamber servant, whose name I do not know, who stroked the ink stone two or three times and then later stole it." The reception envoy ordered the arrest of the suspect, a chamber servant from Yangdŏk 陽德, and had him turned over to the custody of the governor for questioning.

The envoys departed and later arrived at Unam-wŏn. They invited the reception envoy and the governor to have lunch with them. They all drank a few rounds of wine before stopping.

At one o'clock in the afternoon, they arrived in Anju and had a banquet

---

95 This is the assistant envoy Wu Ximeng.

at Paeksang-nu. The envoys arrived at the banquet in their palanquins. The reception envoy, the governor, and the banquet host Chŏng Paekpung 鄭百朋 each greeted them in turn. The envoys sat with their backs to the river, having commanded that their seats be moved so they faced to the south. The reception envoy and the others opened the banquet in the east courtyard and provided female entertainers. The banquet host raised his cup to the envoys and then the reception envoy. The other did the same.

In the evening, the envoys approached the railing and sat comfortably facing the reception envoy and the others, talking quietly. The topic of eunuchs came up and the envoys asked about the origins of eunuchs in this country. Yi Hwajong and the others replied, "This country does not perform castrations. Let us say that a boy is born to a commoner household and the family goes out for some reason [and leaves the baby at home].[96] The baby is swaddled in a blanket, but if it has a bowel movement and is completely covered in feces, dogs will come and as they lick the baby clean, they might bite off the penis and eat it. Generally, it is through accidents like this that eunuchs come to be in this country."

---

96 The source text reads, "…the whole family goes out together" (一家俱出) but the line should be understood as indicating that the baby is left unattended at home while the family is out, as was common practice at the time. I am grateful to Professor Lee Jonghan 李鍾漢 for this explanation.

The envoys did not believe this story and asked the reception envoy and the others if Yi was trying to fool them, but they all said, "It is just as Hwajong said," and added, "Eunuchs from this country who became palace eunuchs (*t'aegam* 太監) in the Central Court, like Chang Hŭm 張欽, Kim Ŭi 金儀, and Chin Ho 陳浩, were all like this."

The envoys began to believe it and said, "The eunuchs in the Central State are different. When the state exacts collective punishment on a criminal and his family, it will castrate rather than execute those sons who have not yet come of age. This is why there are so many eunuchs. The palace eunuch Zhang Qin (K. Chang Hŭm) was an accomplished calligrapher and an able writer. The court placed great trust in him."

As the sun set, [the staff] set torches along the riverbank that were reflected in the water like golden pillars. The envoys leaned against the pillars and summoned the reception envoy, They watched the reflections together in great happiness before the evening came to an end.

May 9, 1537

(4/1)

Clear.

At seven o'clock in the morning, the envoys took their seats in the main hall and ate together. The reception envoy and the governor entered and greeted the envoys before reporting, "We were unable to maintain discipline among the staff and someone has stolen your ink stone. We are mortified."

The assistant envoy laughed and said, "Why have you bothered to report such a minor incident? My own staff have not been vigilant, so this is their fault. With all this fuss, we did not know who stole it, but now, suddenly, there is a suspect. This is even worse [than the theft itself]. If you [casually] assign blame to this person for a vague crime and then at the end omit the name of the thief and carry out [the punishment], it would be the pinnacle of carelessness. The minister certainly wishes to report this quickly to His Majesty, but how could I keep my mind at ease? I would not be able to write poems or engage in jovial banter on the road."[97]

---

97 The envoy does not want the reception envoy to exact punishment on an innocent party for the sake of pleasing him.

The banquet host informed the envoys of his departure. They wrote one poem for him to give to His Majesty. They also each wrote a poem for the banquet host and the governor. The old precedent called for the governor of P'yŏngan Province to accompany the celestial envoys as far as Anju, so Governor Yi Kwiryŏng informed them of his departure. They joked with him, "The governor of Hwanghae Province accompanied us [all the way] to the [provincial] border. How is it that you alone want to go back so soon? We envoys who have traveled ten-thousand *li* do not dare to long for home, but at this point you have been on the road for only three or four days. Why are you thinking of home? You must accompany us to Kasan 嘉山, and then we will release you!"

The governor replied, "There are local administrative issues upon which I must report [to the throne], so I wish to go, but now that I have now heard your lofty command; how could I dare not to honor it?"[98]

The envoys departed and arrived at the Ch'ŏngch'on River. There they boarded an official yacht and summoned the reception envoy and the governor have a drink with them. They quietly chatted with one another. When [the envoys] asked about the line of successive states that preceded

98 Gong Yongqing may have actually been irritated by the governor. See Ŏ Sukkwŏn, "P'aegwan chapki," 141; O Sukkwŏn, *Storyteller's Miscellany*, 193.

this one,[99] starting from Kija, the reception envoy instructed the interpreter to give them a general outline. The chief envoy turned to the assistant envoy and said, "I already know in some detail about the rise and fall of the 'Three Kingdoms.'" He proceeded to give an extremely detailed account of the rise of Chumong 朱蒙, Onjo 溫祚, and Hyŏkkŏse 赫居世.[100] He told the interpreter, "These historical events are known in the Central State and have been recorded in history texts; that is why I know about them well as I do." He added, "According to the vernacular account of the local people from my region, Wang Kŏn, founder of the Koryŏ (高麗) Kingdom was from Changle Prefecture (Changle-xian 長樂縣) in Fujian and his descendants ruled Koryŏ for five-hundred years. They also say that the Chen (V. Trần 陳), the royal family of Annam, also came from Fujian."

Then they asked, "Does your country hold rites for Wang Kŏn?"

"Rites are held at Sungŭi-jŏn 崇義殿 in Majŏn County (Majŏn-gun 麻田郡)," [we replied.]

---

99 "This one," meaning Chosŏn.

100 Chumong was the founder of the Koguryŏ Kingdom, Onjo was the founder of the Paekche Kingdom, and Hyŏkkŏse was the founder of the Silla Kingdom. See Kim Pusik, *Samguk sagi* (Sŏul: Minjok Munhwa Ch'ujinhoe, 1973), 1:1a-4a, 13:1a-5a, 23:1a-7b; Iryŏn, *Chŭngbo samguk yusa*, 40-45; Kim Pusik, "Sage King Tongmyŏng" in *The Koguryŏ Annals of the Samguk Sagi*, trans. Kenneth H. J. Gardiner *et al* (Seongnam, Korea: The Academy of Korean Studies Press, 2011), 37-44; Kim Pusik, "Kŏsŏgan Hyŏkkŏse" in *The Silla Annals of the Samguk Sagi* trans. Kenneth H. J. Gardiner *et al* (Seongnam, Korea: The Academy of Korean Studies Press, 2013), 23-30.

"This is meaningful," they replied.

Then envoys further inquired, "Does your country have the books *Shiji* 史記, *Hanshu* 漢書, *Sanguo zhi* 三國志, *Jinshu* 晉書, *Suishu* 隋書, *Tangshu* 唐書, *Wenxian tongkao* 文獻通考, and *Shiwen leiju* 事文類聚?"

The host office replied, "We have all of them, but we only have the old Koryŏ edition of *Munwŏn yonghwa* (C. *Wenyuan yinghua* 文苑英華), but many portions are missing. His Majesty wishes to print a new edition to distribute widely through the capital and provinces, so he commanded [our] tribute envoys to purchase a copy while they were at the Central Court. They brought back a hand-written manuscript so there are many omissions. Are official editions really so rare in the capital?"[101]

The envoys replied, "This text was compiled during the Song Dynasty and consists of one-hundred volumes. It is difficult to get a complete set. Even we do not have one in our house. I heard about someone who bought a set from a man in Yunnan 雲南 for fifteen taels (*liang* 兩), thinking it cheap. If the king wants to read it, why not send a memorial to the [Ming] throne asking for a complete set?"

The reception envoy asked about the principle governing tides. The

101 The capital here is Beijing.

chief envoy replied, "*Qi* 氣 governs it in much the same fashion as a person breathes."

"Why are there no tides in the East Sea (Tonghae 東海)?"

The chief envoy explained, "The land in the east is inclined so the water is contained, like a full bowl, so there are no tides."

The reception envoy asked the assistant envoy, "What is the meaning of the character *ŏm* 罨 in Ŏmhwa Lake (C. Yanhua-xi罨畫溪) in Sangju (C. Changzhou 常州)?"

He replied, "It is the same as *yan* 掩 (K. *ŏm*), [to hide, to conceal]."

The reception envoy asked the chief envoy, "What is the climate and geography of Fujian like?"

The chief envoy explained, "Fuzhou 福州 is on the coast of the great sea. The people's houses are all built on heights. The water tends to cover half of the flats [so no one can build there]. The weather is always warm and beautiful; flowers bloom throughout all four seasons. And they are all fruit-bearing. Households take pleasure in planting pine, plum, and bamboo. The people do not wear coats because the weather is always warm. After my first official appointment, I was unable to return to my hometown, but I had to return briefly for the funeral of my grandfather. When the funeral was over, I returned to the capital. A mere four months later, I received the commission to come here. My mother is at home and there are five brothers, including myself, but my eldest brother died young. The rest of us, however, are all licentiates (*xiucai* 秀才)."

The envoys also discussed an anthology of poetry from different periods, saying, "The scholars of the Central Court took pleasure in reading [the poetry of] Li Bai 李白, Du Fu 杜甫, and Yuan Zhen 元稹."

In the afternoon, the envoys crossed the Pakch'ŏn River and went up to Konggang-jŏng 控江亭. They invited the reception envoy and the governor to join them for their meal and drinks. They saw a plaque mounted in the pavilion and asked, "Who wrote this? The calligraphy is excellent!"

"That is the calligraphy of Yu Ison 柳耳孫, who has come along with us."

The envoys immediately invited Yu Ison to join them. They gave him some meat and fish and said, "We have seen your face, but we had no idea of your talent for calligraphy."[102]

On the way to Kasan, the envoys saw a large rock standing by itself to the left of the road. They descended from their palanquins and for quite some time they stood by the stone, running their hands over it. In the

102 See Ŏ Sukkwŏn, "P'aegwan chapki," 145; Ŏ Sukkwŏn, *Storyteller's Miscellany*, 214.

evening, they reached Kasan. The banquet was held in Chesan-jŏng 齊山亭. After the banquet, the envoys summoned the archers and had them shoot at targets. The envoys had brought the chamber servant from Anju, Paek Such'ŏn 白壽千 here and they had him recite *The Great Learning* (*Taehak* 大學) as they listened.

May 10, 1537
(4/2)
Clear.

At seven o'clock in the morning, the envoys took their seats at Chesan-jŏng. Once the host envoy and the governor greeted them, the governor informed them of his departure and left. The envoys departed and later arrived at Napch'ŏng-jŏng. They invited the reception envoy to eat with them, instructing the interpreter to say, "When we had the banquet at Kŭnjŏn-jŏn, we said to His Majesty, 'This beautiful gathering was truly not easy to achieve. We ask that a painting be made for the occasion that we can have.' His Majesty approved the request, but the painting has not yet arrived. Minister, please inform the king quickly on my behalf."

The reception envoy replied, "The road is long and difficult, I fear it will not be possible."

The envoys said, "If that is the case, send it to the commander at Tangzhan, Han Chengqing 韓承慶, and instruct him to send it on to Liaodong. We will speak with him before we go." They then ordered the archers to shoot targets, saying to the reception envoy, "Sŏ Myŏngch'ŏn 徐命千 from the minister's household and the Yongch'ŏn County Magistrate (*Yŏngch'ŏn kunsu* 龍泉君守) Cho Sebong 曺世鳳 are superb archers. You should inform His Majesty."

In the evening, they reached Chŏngju and postponed the banquet until the following morning. One of the chief envoy's attendants became angry with a chamber servant and punched him. Another one accused a post station slave of losing his flute and demanded he find it and give it back. The chief envoy heard about this and had the attendants arrested and beaten with a staff as punishment.

The chief envoy wrote a short note which read:

> The [name of the person] you mentioned, "Han Eighteen," refers to his birth order among his brothers. Now, the large

> families in the Central State have brothers that number in the tens, hundreds, or even thousands. For those who were born in different years, in different months, on different days, and different hours, one can know the birth order but for those who were born in the same month, on the same day, and at the same time – how can one tell them apart? In this way, the order of the brothers is determined by the time and date of their birth. The birth order then determines who is older and how is younger, without the slightest error. One can know who is older and who is younger without even asking for ages. They start from [the number] one and continue. Whether there are tens, hundreds, or thousands of brothers, all the families are like this. In Du Fu's poems, Gao Thirty-Five (Gao Sanshiwu 高三十五), Xu Eleven (Xu Shiyi 許十一), and Cui Nine (Cui Jiu 崔九) are all examples of this. Grandfathers have a grandfather order, fathers have a father order, and sons have a son order, and none of them violate their respective orders. This is the meaning of the line from *The Doctrine of the Mean* (Zhongyong 中庸), "At the banquet, hair determines the order of years."[103]

The chief envoy wrote another note that read:

103 This refers to the seating arrangement at a banquet where guests are seating according to age. Hair color, from black to grey to white, determines the order. See "Zhongyong" in *Xinchu jingjiao sishu buzhu beizhi* ed. Deng Lin (Shanghai: Tianbao Shuju, 1916), 1:10a. This entire passage appears in a slightly abridged form in Ŏ Sukkwŏn, "P'aegwan chapki," 149; Ŏ Sukkwŏn, *Storyteller's Miscellany*, 237.

> When preparing oysters, you must never discard the natural oyster juice. If you just boil them in water, they will not taste good. With this method, mix with a generous amount of pork fat and when the oil is boiling, add the oysters and stir them with a spoon. When then are about done, add some alcohol or some batter and mix it together. Even if you are only using batter, it is important to add a little alcohol to temper the fishy odor. Not too much, not too little. It has to be just right before you can eat it. For the best taste, you really must use some alcohol, even if it is just a little bit to cut the fishiness. Generally, if seafood smells rotten once it has met with a southerly wind (nanfeng 南風),[104] you cannot eat it. In fact, it is dangerous. There are several ways to boil oysters. The way I have just described is excellent, but aside from this method, they can also be simmered in the shell, steamed in the shell, or removed from the shell and batter-fried. These are all very good methods. Oysters are among the best products of the sea so you must know how to prepare them.[105]

The chief envoy wrote another note that read, "Whenever the minister has asked a question, I have always answered truthfully. We both properly understand the fundamental beauty and grace of the way. How could

---

104 A southerly wind is a warm wind. The implication here is that seafood easily rots in warm weather.

105 This recipe can be found in nearly identical form in Ŏ Sukkwŏn, "P'aegwan chapki," 149-150; Ŏ Sukkwŏn, *Storyteller's Miscellany*, 237-8.

there be any ill will or suspicion between us?" He also said, "The proper etiquette for walking is as follows: When exiting [a doorway], the higher [status person should be] to the east side of the threshold; when entering [a doorway], the higher [status person should be] to the west side of the threshold. You must not overlook these details."[106]

May 11, 1537
(4/3)
Clear.

At five o'clock in the morning, the envoys took their seats in the main hall, and the reception envoy entered and greeted them. The envoys said, "Today the road will be long and difficult so you need not prepare a banquet." They then departed, later arriving at Unhŭng-gwan where they had lunch. They had lunch [again] at Imban-gwan. During the meal, the

106 The content of these two notes appears in nearly identical form in Ŏ Sukkwŏn, "P'aegwan chapki," 149; Ŏ Sukkwŏn, *Storyteller's Miscellany*, 237. This appears to be an instruction to Chŏng as to where to walk when entering and exiting buildings. Gong Yongqing seems to have had this conversation with other Chosŏn officials as well. See *Chungjong sillok*, 32/3/12.

envoys asked, "Where is the minister?" They wanted to have lunch with him.

The interpreter responded, "Unaware of the grandfathers' command, the minister has already eaten on his own."

The envoys said, "In three or four days, we will have to part. From now on, he must eat with us whenever we stop to rest." As the sun began to set, they reached Kŏryŏn-gwan and postponed the banquet.

May 12, 1537
(4/4)
Clear.

The envoys took their seats in the main hall, and the reception envoy entered and greeted them. He then presented them with a sea otter pelt. The envoys whispered into one another's ears and then said, "We have already experienced the sincere hospitality of His Majesty. Now we are speechless! It was already not entirely proper to have accepted the ink stone. Now this is all the more so! We have been traveling together with the minister for many days now. How could he not know our thinking on such matters?" They waved the pelt away while the reception envoys pleaded repeatedly with them. The envoys, however, refused to accept it.

The envoys departed after breakfast and later arrived at Yangch'aek-kwan where they had lunch. When they crossed the Kojin River (Kojin-gang 古津江), they sat in chairs on the stone bridge and watched the water. They later reached Sogok-kwan and had lunch [again]. They arrived at Ŭisun-gwan at three-o'clock in the afternoon and instructed that the banquet be postponed until the following day.

The Liaodong Censor sent a troupe of fourteen performers who had already arrived [at Ŭisun-gwan] and were waiting. Also, Regional Commander Li Jingliang 李景良 had arrived at Posuo-bao 婆娑堡[107] with 1,500 men under his command. He dispatched two battalion commanders and four platoon commanders to meet the envoys and inquire as to their welfare.

---

107 Posuo-bao was a Ming fortification near the Yalu River frontier with Chosŏn.

May 13, 1537

(4/5)

Clear.

The envoys stayed at Ŭisun-gwan. The chief envoy commanded the interpreter to say to the reception envoy, "We have been traveling quickly and are exhausted. We wish to stay for two or three days and then cross the Amnok River on May 15 (4/7) or May 16 (4/8). The painting *Banquet at Kŭnjŏng-jŏn* has not yet arrived despite the king's approval. Why has it yet to arrive? If it does not arrive before we cross the river, we will talk with the commander at Tangzhan. Once the painting is completed and arrives here, send it to Tangzhan and have it forwarded on to Liaodong." He also said, "The publication of *Chaoxian fu* 朝鮮賦[108] is not yet complete but after we return to Beijing it will be printed. Then we will have the provincial military commander see that it is sent to your country."

At seven o'clock in the morning, the envoys took their seats in the main hall and summoned the reception envoy to eat with them. He then

108 Ming envoy Dong Yue wrote this account of his mission to Chosŏn in 1488.

explained the whole Hyŏpgang 夾江 Incident from start to finish.[109] The envoys replied, "We heard about this incident in detail when we were still at court. Censor Yang Xingzhong 楊行中 said, 'The Jiajiang 夾江 (K. Hyŏpgang) incident is really a matter of common sense. The border must be well demarcated and all the rules must be enforced. Last year when I was on an inspection tour of Liaodong, this matter had already been settled.' When we arrived in Liaoyang 遼陽, Censor Shi Dao 史道 spoke to us about this matter and his opinion the same as that of Censor Yang. The Censor-in-Chief of Guangning said to us, 'The king of Chosŏn respectfully serves the [Ming] court. Whenever someone [from Ming] runs away [to Chosŏn], [the king] pays his travel expenses and sends him back. Never has he lapsed in his concern. This is a worthiness to be praised. If no one submits a memorial to the throne to praise these actions, how can others be encouraged to goodness?' When we return from this mission, we will speak to the censors of Liaodong and Guangning to draft a prohibition on farming in Jiajiang."

---

109 There are a number of islands and river channels in the lower reaches of the Yalu River. The Chosŏn-Ming boundary was not always clear in this area so Ming and Chosŏn farmers often came into contact and conflict. These confrontations could sometimes turn violent. While Chŏng Saryong is speaking about the "start and finish" of the incident, many problems arose between Chosŏn and Ming farmers in this area between 1535 and 1544. The particular incident of which Chŏng most likely spoke is reported in some detail in *Chungjong sillok* 30/8/10.

The reception envoy spoke about the past matter of Kim Tongnan 金同難.[110] "The reason Kim Tongnan can commit all these crimes is that there are so many people furtively living close to both sides of the frontier who secretly move back and forth across the border."

The envoys said, "We already know about this situation in detail."

The reception envoy was going to take his leave, but the chief envoy grabbed him by the hand and said, "After we part, there will be no reason for the minister to see me again. And what opportunity will I have to see the minister again? When I think of this, I come to realize just how miserable I am."

[We] had the interpreter Hong Kyŏm report to the envoys that *Palace Examination Questions* (*Chŏnsich'aek* 殿試策) and *Roster of Successful Examinees* (*Tŭnggwa pangmok* 登科榜目) had arrived from the capital. The envoys looked through them and said, "We greatly appreciate His Majesty thinking of us from afar, but why only these two?"

Hong Kyŏm replied, "If I present one, the other three can be

110 Kim Tongnan of Ŭiju was a notorious thief, cattle rustler, and accomplished con-man who often crossed the frontier and engaged in a variety of crimes from the late 1520s until the early 1540s. He was a constant source of irritation in Chosŏn-Ming relations. For the first of his many appearances in the records of the Chosŏn court, see *Chungjong sillok* 23/5/16.

known."[111]

The chief envoy said, "You are a literate man."

At eleven o'clock in the morning, Provincial Inspector and Hospitality envoy Cho In'gyu went to Kŏmdong Island (Kŏmdong-do 黔同島)[112] to prepare a banquet [for the envoys.]

In the evening, there was a banquet in the main hall. The reception envoy, banquet host Yi Hŭibo 李希輔, Special Banquet Host Pak Suryang entered, greeted the envoys, and took their seats. The reception envoy instructed the interpreter to report to the envoys, "Provincial Inspector and Hospitality envoy Cho In'gyu is here." The envoys called upon him to commence the banquet and commanded the entertainers who came from Liaodong to begin their performance amidst the tables. Secretary (*sŭngji* 承旨) Pak first raised his cup [to the envoys] and then the reception envoy and the others each did so in turn. The banquet was over in the early evening. Yi Hŭibo and Pak Suryang informed the envoys that they would depart. The envoys said, "You do not wish to see us off at the river? Also, we wish to send a letter to His Majesty. Wait one day and then come back and we will

---

111 Hong Kyŏm is making a reference here to a passage in *The Analects* in which Confucius says that if he presents one corner of a subject and his student cannot understand the other three, he will not repeat the lesson again. See "Shu er" in *Xinchu jingjiao sishu buzhu beizhi*, 2:8a.

112 Kŏmdong Island is in the Yalu River.

instruct you."

On this day, [we] instructed Yi Hwajong to deliver the large and small ink stones that the celestial envoys had wanted. The medium one had been ordered the day before and was not yet ready so it could not yet be presented.

May 14, 1537

(4/6)

Clear.

The envoys stayed in Ŭiju. The reception envoy sent a paper bird and flower arrangement (*kŭmsabong* 金絲鳳) to each envoy because when they were previously in Pyŏkche-gwan, they had asked for one. The envoys said, "We were not really serious, and yet you did not forget!" They each took three branches and said, "This is enough." The envoys then said to the interpreter, "Since we traveled so quickly, there is some extra time. We are exhausted and wish to stay another day. The minister need not rush us. Today, suspend the banquet."

May 15, 1537

(4/7)

Rain.

The envoys stayed in Ŭiju. At eleven o'clock in the morning, the extended-stay banquet began. The envoys took their seats and the reception envoy and the others each offered wine.

The chief envoy produced more than ten more poems that he had written on the road and sent them to the reception envoy. And then he instructed the hospitality envoy and the others to write poems in response. Yi Hŭibo and Pak Suryang each wrote two or three poems before they informed the envoys of their regrettable departure. The chief envoy said to the interpreter, "How is it that the scholars of your country all write so well? From this it is easy to tell the abundance of human talent." He also asked, "Only the officers of the Reception Commission did not write poems. Why is that?"

The interpreter replied, "Although they are civil officials, they do not understand composition, so they do not dare to try."

The envoys turned to another and said, "Why are they all so careful?"

The envoys wrote farewell poems and sent them to the reception envoy, the banquet host, and various assistants.

The assistant envoy gave a copy of *A Survey of Stars and Masts* (*Xingcha shenglan* 星槎勝覽),[113] Xia Yan's *Memorials on the Suburban Rites* (*Jiaosi zuoyi* 郊祀奏議), and *Memorials on Contemporary Administration* (*Shizheng zouyi* 時政奏議) to the reception envoy and said, "This is my only copy of *A Survey of Stars and Masts*. Copy it out tonight and then send the original to Tang-zhan."

May 15, 1537

(4/8)

Clear.

At seven o'clock in the morning, the envoys took their seats in the main hall and summoned the reception envoy and the banquet host to join them for breakfast. When the meal was finished, they departed and later arrived at the banquet hall on the river. The envoys had written farewell poems

---

113 This is an account of the fifteenth-century exploratory voyages of Zheng He 鄭和 as written by one of his officers, Fei Xin 費信.

for all the staff and all the chief magistrates along the entire route of the embassy. They also gave letters to the secretary and told him to deliver them to the king. The envoys then took their seats. Once the reception envoy and the banquet host had each offered wine, the envoys each drank one cup. Then they urged the reception envoy, members of the staff, the P'yŏngan provincial inspector, and the magistrate of Ŭiju to do the same. And then the banquet was over. Yi Hŭibo and Pak Suryang informed the envoys of their departure and left. The envoys then boarded their palanquins.

The farewell envoy (*pansongsa* 伴送使) lead the whole entourage to the Amnok River. There were tables set on the boat and they drank several rounds. They envoys turned and looked back with tears in their eyes. The tried to speak but could not. The chief envoy was of a miserable countenance and instructed the interpreter to say to the farewell envoy, "In the future, when the next [Chosŏn] tributary envoy comes, be sure to send a letter with him. And if I am outside the capital on official business, then Mr. Wu will be there. And if Mr. Wu has left the capital, I will be there." And with that, he began to sob uncontrollably. And then everyone, from the farewell envoy on down to the slaves, all began to cry. The farewell envoy and staff offered wine and the envoys summoned the entire entourage to drink, saying to the farewell envoy, "His Majesty the king has been utterly sincere for the [Ming] court above and utterly devoted for us below. When we return to court, how can we ever forget our longing [for the king], even for a single day? Be sure to report our inexhaustible affection to His Majesty.

The boat reached the north bank. Regional Commander Li Jingliang was waiting at the riverside. The envoys summoned him aboard and the minister, staff, and the interpreter all bowed. [We] requested the whole entourage to disembark first and then wait on the shore. Then the envoys and the regional commander stepped onto the shore. The minister and the whole entourage bowed twice to the envoys who saluted in return. Then [the minister and the entourage] took their leave and returned to the boat. The envoys entered the regional commander's banquet hall, instructing their attendants Gao Song and Kang Zhen to go to the farewell envoy and say, "It is appropriate [for you] to cross the river now. We will watch the minister return and then we will leave."

When they crossed the river on this day, the members of the envoys' households requested the woven beaded blinds and leopard skins from the palanquins. [We] gave them immediately. The envoys expressed their gratitude for the horses supplied earlier in the capital.

The envoys came to the river bank and waved, telling the farewell envoy's boat to go but [the crew] just kept the boat by the shore, not moving. Finally, the farewell envoy and his entourage boarded their boat. By this time the sun was already setting. They envoys stood far outside their banquet hall, looking toward this shore with their hands clasped in a farewell salute. The farewell envoy and the others clasped their hands in response and once the envoys departed, they returned.

[We] instructed the magistrate of Ŭiju to store the gifts the Ministry of Rites had sent to Gao Song and the other attendants until such time as he could send them to Liaodong with the next envoy to express gratitude for imperial grace.

Travel Log of the Celestial Envoys: Translator's Introduction

On March 30, 1537, Chief Proclamation Envoy Gong Yongqing 龔用卿, Assistant Proclamation Envoy Wu Ximeng 吳希盟, and their entourage of interpreters and attendants arrived on the north bank of the Amnok River, the frontier between Ming China and Chosŏn Korea. The Ming court had dispatched them to deliver the formal proclamation of the birth of the Ming imperial crown prince to the Chosŏn royal court. On the Chosŏn shore, Reception Envoy Chŏng Saryong 鄭士龍, the interpreters Yi Hwajong 李和宗 and Hong Kyŏm 洪謙, and many other staff members of the Chosŏn Reception Commission (*wŏnjŏp togam* 遠接都監) waited for the envoys to make their crossing. This was the beginning of a six-week journey from the Amnok River south to Seoul and back again to the river, during which time Chŏng, the commission staff, and the Chosŏn provincial governors and local magistrates along the entire route were responsible for ensuring that every need of the envoys was met and their every demand satisfied.

As a tributary state to the Ming court, the Chosŏn government made every effort to host the Ming envoys flawlessly. While the reception envoy and his staff engaged in little direct discussion of Chosŏn-Ming diplomacy, it was of critical diplomatic importance to the Chosŏn court that the Reception Commission ensure that the Ming envoys had good experiences in Chosŏn and returned home with new friendships and happy memories. Each Ming envoy that returned home impressed with Chosŏn hospitality was a potential advocate of Chosŏn state interests at the Ming court. *Travel Log of the Celestial Envoys* is the daily record of the Reception Commission's hosting of the Ming envoys, covering nearly every day that they were in Chosŏn territory. As the Reception Commission was responsible for ensuring the envoys' complete satisfaction, this log of its efforts is something of a transparent, and perhaps institutionally self-serving, declaration of a job well done.

Travel Log of the Celestial Envoys covers a remarkable variety of activities and issues of Reception Commission during its six-week assignment. From the outset of the log, ceremonial protocols are a central area of concern. There were formal banquets nearly every day of the journey and the log meticulously records the ceremonial protocols involved, including bows, salutes, the offering of alcohol, the drinking of alcohol, and the preparation of fruit plates, soups, and seafood. While the early banquets appear to have been free of contention, there were often cases in which the protocols, always decided in advance, were the subject of some debate between the Ming envoys and their Chosŏn hosts. The Reception Commission presented a program for the banquets, including seating arrangements and entertainment, to the envoys in the form of "ceremonial notes" (*ŭiju* 儀註) for prior approval. The log records several of the sometimes tense conversations between the envoys and their hosts concerning which precedents were to inform the conduct of these events.

Many days on the road included entertainment in various forms, including archery demonstrations, competitions, and games of *t'uho* 投壺 in which players attempt to toss arrows into narrow openings in a vase or similar container in a manner reminiscent of the game cornhole. The envoys were also fond of drinking games, guessing games, and games that combined both drinking and guessing. There were performances of music and dance by both Ming and Chosŏn performers. As I will discuss below, performances by female musicians and dancers were a frequent point of contention. While the envoys often protested the provision of female performers, they clearly took great pleasure in them, a predilection that led to crude behavior deeply humiliating to the Chosŏn court.

Like other Ming envoys, Gong and Wu wrote a great deal of poetry as they traveled through northwest Chosŏn, or at least they produced a great deal of poetry about their journey in Chosŏn, even if some portion of the poetry may have been composed in advance.[114] The log records little of the content of the poetry but rather chronicles the prodigious output and the repeated demands the envoys issued to commit their verse to wooden plaques to be mounted in the various pavilions and halls about which they had written. Indeed, they often found the existing names of the buildings they visited or the landscape features they enjoyed to be, in one way or another, insufficient and took to renaming the Chosŏn natural and built environment.[115] The log shows on several occasions the headache this predilection became for Chŏng Saryong and the provincial officials along the envoys' route.

Some of the most engaging portions of the log are the transcripts of conversations between Chosŏn officials and the envoys. The envoys have numerous questions about Chosŏn civil service examinations, history, culture, language, flora and fauna, and food. Chŏng Saryong asks the envoys about Tang poetry and poets, Chinese historical sites, language, and

---

114 Ŏ Sukkwŏn, "P'aegwan chapki," in *Taedong yasŭng* vol. 1, (Sŏul: Kyŏnghŭi Ch'ulp'ansa, 1968), 142; O Sukkwŏn, *A Korean Storyteller's Miscellany* trans. Peter H. Lee (Princeton: Princeton University Press, 1989), 196-7; Sixiang Wang, *Boundless Winds of Empire: Rhetoric and Ritual in Early Chosŏn Diplomacy with Ming China* (New York: Columbia University Press, 2023), 207.

115 Ŏ Sukkwŏn, "P'aegwan chapki," 151; Ŏ Sukkwŏn, *Storyteller's Miscellany*, 244.

geography. In reading these conversations, which took place either through interpreters or in writing, one gets the sense that the Chosŏn hosts may have been humoring the envoys as they droned on about this or that point of their personal interests but there are times when Chŏng Saryong, in particular, makes inquiries of his own about Chinese language and literature studies that convey something of his intellectual interests and scholarly spirit.

Given the broad array of subject matter included in the *Travel Log*, the question arises as to who may have compiled it and by what means. The manuscript upon which the present translation is based indicates neither an author nor a compiler. The text itself is similarly bereft of any substantive clues to its authorship. Chang Injin 張仁鎭 notes in his description of the manuscript in the Keimyung University Dongsan Library catalog that the log is devoid of any first person pronouns that might signal authorship. This leads Chang to speculate, not unreasonably, that the log was compiled by lower-ranking officers under the order of Chŏng Saryong, perhaps Pak Ch'ungwŏn 朴忠元 or Hong Ch'un'gyŏng 洪春卿.[116] Kim Yunjo 金允朝,

116 Kim Yunjo, "*Ch'ŏnsa illo ilgi* haeje" in Chŏng Saryong et al. comp., *Ch'ŏnsa illo ilgi: Chosŏn, myŏng nara sasin ŭl matta*, trans. Kim Yunjo, Yi Chian, and Hwang Tonggwŏn (Taegu: Kyemyŏng Taehakkyo Ch'ulp'anbu, 2020), 194.

one of the translators of the recent modern Korean translation, suggests that Chŏng Saryong either wrote the log himself, or had it compiled by his underlings, in some fashion was responsible for its compilation. Kim makes his proposal on the inclusion of Chŏng's personal anecdotes in some of the log entries.[117] While it is entirely reasonable to expect that Chŏng, in his capacity as the reception envoy, had an important role to play in the production of the log, it seems unlikely that he did it himself. As Chang Injin suggests, he may well have had those under his command do the actual work of compilation, subject to his editing or final approval. Moreover, the presence of Chŏng's personal anecdotes does not indicate his authorship as they are commonplace reported speech. The log is replete with the reported speech of many people who were either members of the Ming embassy, the Reception Commission staff, or others who were not present at all.

There is, however, another candidate beyond Chŏng Saryong, Pak Ch'ungwŏn, and Hong Ch'un'gyŏng. Ŏ Sukkwŏn 魚叔權 (fl. 1525-1554) was an interpreter who participated both in Chosŏn missions to Ming and the 1537 Ming mission to Chosŏn.[118] He was member of the Chosŏn entourage

---

117 Kim Yunjo, "*Ch'ŏnsa illo ilgi* haeje," 194-6.
118 Ŏ Sukkwŏn, *Storyteller's Miscellany*, ix-x, xiii-xv, 3.

in his capacity as a diplomatic drafting officer (*imunhakkwan* 吏文學官) from the Office of Diplomatic Correspondence (*Sŭngmunwŏn* 承文院).[119] His primary duty in this post was to draft documents related to foreign relations. From this fact alone, his involvement in the compilation of the *Travel Log* would seem probable, but there is further evidence. Ŏ is well-known for his collection of engaging anecdotes entitled, *P'aegwan chapki* 稗官雜記. Ŏ curated many of the anecdotes included therein from his personal experiences as a diplomatic interpreter and drafter. *P'aegwan chapki* contains numerous events and conversations that also appear in the *Travel Log*, as seen in the entries for April 8, 10, 13, 16, May 2, 6, and 9. This would suggest that Ŏ had some kind of connection or contact with the log. Moreover, there are several instances in which materials in the log and in his collection of anecdotes are nearly identical, as can be seen in the entry for May 10.

The strongest piece of evidence suggesting that Ŏ Sukkwŏn was a compiler, if not the compiler, of the *Travel Log* is a case of misinterpretation at Tongp'a-gwan 東坡館. On April 16, 1537, the envoys arrived at Tongp'a-gwan on their way to Seoul. The chief envoy asked that blank scrolls be prepared for him and his colleague to write the poetry

---

119 *Chungjong sillok* 32/4/30.

they had written on the road once they arrived in Seoul. When the envoys were on their way back to Beijing, they again stopped at Tongp'a-gwan, this time on April 27. That night Ŏ Sukkwŏn and the interpreter Hong Kyŏm shared a room. Ŏ Sukkwŏn wrote in *P'aegwan chapki* that they called for a lamp in order to compile an unidentified "log" (余與譯士洪謙同宿呼燈撰次日記). As they worked, Hong Kyŏm read the entry for April 16 in which Gong Yongqing commanded the preparation of blank scrolls.[120] Hong said that the Chosŏn interpreter, Yi Hwajong, had misunderstood Gong who had in fact commanded the fabrication of wooden plaques for their verse, not blank scrolls. The content Hong read appears to be substantively the same as that in the April 16 entry in the *Travel Log*, suggesting that Ŏ, and perhaps Hong as well, were working on its compilation.

In his English translation of *P'aegwan chapki*, Peter Lee identified this log (*ilgi* 日記) as Ŏ's personal diary[121] but this seems unlikely. The verb *ch'anch'a* 撰次 means literally to compile or to collect (撰) disparate parts or materials and put them into order (次). A more likely scenario is that Ŏ was collecting written materials from that day and arranging them into a log entry. The materials may well have come from the Chosŏn interpreters, of whom

120 Ŏ Sukkwŏn, "P'aegwan chapki," 137; Ŏ Sukkwŏn, *Storyteller's Miscellany*, 174.
121 Ŏ Sukkwŏn, *Storyteller's Miscellany,* 3, 174.

Hong Kyŏm was one, or perhaps from Chŏng Saryong, or from any of the other Chosŏn officials who may have had written conversations with the envoys and their attendants. If this were the case, it would go some distance in accounting for the frequently disjointed and telegraphic nature of the *Travel Log*. There is no consistent narrative structure, only a cataloging of short observations or dialogues. Additionally, the fact that Hong would have only seen the April 16 entry on April 27 suggests that he did not have regular access to the log draft. This possibly indicates that Ŏ was the sole compiler, or at least the regular compiler. As his primary duty was to draft documents related to foreign relations, his *P'aegwan chapki* shares content with the *Travel Log*, and the *P'aegwan chapki* makes specific reference to his being on this mission and compiling a log with the participation of the interpreter Hong Kyŏm, it seems highly probably that Ŏ Sukkwŏn was the compiler of *Ch'ŏnsa illo ilgi*.

Admittedly, these bits of evidence do not prove this decisively, and Chang Injin's assertion that the log was compiled under Chŏng Saryong's direction is imminently acceptable. We might do well to remember that this document is not a collection of personal observations, or even a record of objective observations, but rather an official document produced with in a particular matrix of potentially competing intragovernmental interests and highly sensitive intergovernmental relationships. Knowledge of individual authorship in this setting may be less important than understanding the production and consumption of the document in institutional context.

In reading *Travel Log of the Celestial Envoys*, the reader is well-advised to keep forefront in the mind it is not record of event so much as it is a textual performance. It is one collective utterance in a larger tributary discourse, a set of rhetorical practices that, to the novice reader, may appear not only as empty and excessive, but bordering on the absurd. Did the Chosŏn officials really understand the celestial envoys as being in some way *celestial*? Did they really believe the Ming Empire and its emperor to be the world font of authentic human civilization and perfected morality? Did the Ming envoys sincerely see themselves as emissaries of imperial virtue, grace, and benevolence? Were they honestly impressed by the manifold instantiations of Chosŏn adherence to ritual propriety? So distant are these rhetorical practices to the present that one may be tempted to dismiss them entirely. In the words of the early twentieth-century American historian Carl Becker, texts so removed from our current time and place appear to the modern reader as "neither true nor false, but only irrelevant."[122]

---

122 Carl Becker, *The Heavenly City of the Eighteenth-Century Philosophers* (New Haven: Yale University Press, 1932), 11-12.

While tributary rhetoric is not to be taken as an objective accounting of the Chosŏn-Ming relationship, it is not to be ignored. It was not a series of statements *about* the Chosŏn-Ming relationship. Tributary discourse *produced* the relationship. It was a performative discursive practice that created the relationship in which it was repeatedly deployed in constant process of production and reproduction over the centuries of the Chosŏn-Ming and Chosŏn-Qing relationships.[123] Understood in this fashion, tributary discourse is no way vapid flourish, empty condescension, or debased flattery. It is central to the working of the Chosŏn-Ming relationship and of critical importance to Chosŏn diplomatic agency with a neighboring empire of incomparable wealth and power. It was within these rhetorical rules that the Chosŏn court was able to maneuver, bending tributary tropes to advocate for its own interests.

We might best understand the central dynamics of the Chosŏn-Ming tributary relationship through the phrase "serve the great, nurture the small" (*sadae chaso* 事大字小). Here the small Chosŏn serves the Great Ming while the Great Ming nurtures the small Chosŏn. At first blush, this

---

123 Joshua Van Lieu. "Chosŏn-Qing Tributary Discourse: Transgression, Restoration, and Textual Performativity," *Cross-Currents: East Asian History and Culture Review* 7 no. 2 (November 2018), 327-329; Wang, *Boundless Winds of Empire*, 43.

arrangement seems nothing more than a patronizing relationship in which the weaker Chosŏn state is locked into abject servitude, if not servility, but a deeper consideration of this ideal pairing suggests that there are mutual obligations. While Chosŏn must serve Ming, Ming must fulfill its duties as well. In his most recent work, Sixiang Wang argues that the mutual obligations in this relationship enabled Chosŏn, through its performative production of tributary discourse, to guide, cajole, and channel Ming policy. It was the very maintenance of the tributary discourse and ritual practice that opened up opportunities for the weaker Chosŏn Kingdom to influence the stronger Ming Empire.[124]

The ways in which the Chosŏn court employed tributary rhetoric and ritual become more apparent through an examination of some of the absences in *Travel Log of the Celestial Envoys*. An interesting element of the log is that there is no record of the activities of the Ming envoys while they were in Seoul. There is a relatively terse account of their initial reception outside the city gates, their presentation of the proclamation, King Chungjong's prostrations before it, and the tea at Kyŏngbok Palace thereafter. The entries for the next six days, however, read only, "[The

---

124 Wang, *Boundless Winds of Empire*, 30-35, 133-4, 283-4.

envoys] stayed in T'aep'yŏng-gwan" (在太平館). While it is true that the envoys did sleep and eat most of their meals at T'aep'yŏng-gwan, they also were busy every day of their stay in Seoul. There were banquets at T'aep'yŏng-gwan, a visit to the Altar to Confucius at the Sŏnggyun-gwan 成均館 Academy, a pleasure cruise on the Han River, a banquet at Kyŏnghoe-ru 慶會樓, and another banquet at Kŭnjŏng-jŏn 勤政殿. The anonymous compiler, or compilers, included none of this in the log. It is hard to know why this is the case. Perhaps the log was meant only to cover the portions of the envoys' journey in which they were on the road. The omissions might also be explained, however, by some of the problems that arose while the envoys were in Seoul. Unlike the relatively smooth interactions between the envoys and Chosŏn officers that characterize the *Travel Log*, there several cases in which the state catering services failed to prepare for hosting the envoys, resulting in insufficient staffing, alcohol, and food. King Chungjong was especially upset by these failures. More serious still, however, were the instances of the appalling behavior on the part of the envoys and the problem of how the Chosŏn court should respond to these incidents. It is in the court discussion of these problems that we can see what the diplomatic stakes for Chosŏn and how the Chosŏn state deployed the rhetoric and ritual of the tributary relationship in its navigation of these incidents for the purpose of advancing its interests.

Lapses in hosting protocols began with the first banquet for the envoys after their arrival, the Dismounting Banquet (*hamayŏn* 下馬宴), on the evening of April 19. The banquet seems to have run out of alcohol and fruit plates, and the director of the Royal Cuisine Office (*Saongwŏn* 司饔院), who was supposed to have been at the king's side at the banquet, failed to show up at all.[125] On April 21, the envoys visited the Altar to Confucius and then proceeded to take a pleasure cruise on the Han River. When they returned to shore, First Royal Secretary Pak Hongnin 朴洪麟[126] wanted fruit plates served to the envoys but there were none. He asked the Reception Commission to serve them but the commission refused, explaining that it was responsible only for the catering on the yacht itself. Pak did not indicate whom he asked but it would be reasonable to suspect that he asked Chŏng Saryong, who was surely present as the reception envoy. His name does not appear among those on the river cruise but the envoys did require his presence at the visit to the Altar to Confucius earlier in the day. Having been refused by the Reception Commission, whether it was Chŏng or

125 *Chungjong sillok* 32/3/11. The *Travel Log* entry for April 19 hardly mentions the dismounting banquet, let alone theses lapses in service.

126 Pak Hongnin's name sometimes appears as 洪麟, sometimes as 洪鱗.

someone else, Pak then instructed the Royal Cuisine Office to supply the fruit plates, but they too refused, explaining that they were responsible only for the formal banquets, and that indeed it was the duty of the Reception Commission to provide the catering for all other entertainment events for the envoys while they were in Seoul. Pak was finally able to convince the Ritual Guest Agency (*Yebinsi* 禮賓寺) serve the envoys.[127]

King Chungjong took these lapses very seriously and had the director of the Royal Cuisine Office arrested and subject to interrogation. Mistakes such as these, he explained would be serious even under normal circumstances, but they were all the more serious in the context of hosting imperial envoys. What concerned the king the most was the possibility that the envoys would read them as evidence that the Chosŏn court did not take its duty to host them seriously. This, the king explained, would cause serious damage to the integrity of the state (大損國體).[128] In short, it was of critical importance that the envoys be impressed with their treatment. It would require more serious hosting challenges before the king would be more specific. The behavior of the envoys would eventually provide those very challenges as the days of their Seoul sojourn passed.

---

127 *Chungjong sillok* 32/3/13.

128 *Chungjong sillok* 32/3/11.

The envoys, and Gong Yongqing in particular, proved very difficult guests. They were prone to disputing ceremonial notes, demanding the provision of all manner of food and supplies, speaking flippantly at moments that required the utmost seriousness and rectitude, and indulging in drunken coarse jokes and outrageously lewd behavior. This made them singularly unpopular among the Chosŏn officials and even among their own entourage.[129] While some of this comes out occasionally in the *Travel Log*, the severity of their boorishness only comes to the fore in the entries of the Chosŏn court records as King Chungjong and his officials repeatedly discussed how best to respond to various excessive demands or sundry violations of decorum great and small.

One of the many arguments over ceremonial notes concerned the crown prince's banquet for the envoys. When the Chosŏn court first issued the crown prince's invitation, the envoys refused on the grounds that there would not be enough time, but after much pleading, the envoys agreed to attend. There was, however, a caveat. Gong Yongqing was explicit that the protocols for the banquet with the crown prince should not be the same as those for the banquet with the king. He wanted to see the ceremonial

---

129 *Chungjong sillok* 32/3/13.

notes in advance to make sure that the banquet would be executed to his satisfaction. Existing Chosŏn precedent, however, made no differentiation between the king's banquet and the crown prince's banquet. Moreover, there was no real differentiation in status between the king and prince in the seating arrangement. The king and prince were to sit together on the west side of the banquet hall while the envoys were to sit on the east side. Protocol Inquiry Officer Im P'irhyŏng 任弼亨 took the existing ceremonial notes with him on the Han River cruise to show to the envoys. The notes were based on existing precedent but did not incorporate Gong's demanded changes. The decision to privilege precedent over contemporary imperatives turned out to be infelicitous.[130]

Gong was furious. Im P'irhyŏng reported that the envoys found the ceremonial notes for the crown prince's banquet utterly unacceptable. Second State Councilor Kim Allo 金安老, who was with the envoys on the Han River cruise, protested Gong's harsh reaction, explaining that the notes simply followed the format of previous crown prince banquets. The prince had not simply made them up himself. Gong was not assuaged. Although he took a slightly conciliatory approach by blaming the interpreters for

130 Im P'irhyŏng's report and the ensuing court discussion can be found in *Chungjong sillok* 32/3/12, 14.

not having expressed his requirements correctly, he did not soften his tone with Kim Allo. There were two points of contention for Gong. The first was that the east-west orientation of the seating arrangement meant that first, there was no differentiation in position between the king and prince, and second, the prince was in a position of higher status than the envoys. Gong pointed out that if the envoys were to sit to the east, they would be facing the prince in the position of honor in the west. As the prince was not the king, and in to Gong's mind, the equivalent of a common man, it was insulting to have to sit in the east across from him. The second point of contention was the use of the generic term "envoy" (*sasin* 使臣) in the notes. Gong complained, "It is not correct to refer to us as 'envoys.' How could anyone who knows ritual be like this?" (亦不當稱我等爲使臣豈知禮者若是), "And why do the ceremonial notes make reference to 'envoys?' This is also unacceptable" (且儀註何以稱使臣乎亦不可也), and "How could it be that the crown prince dares to refer to proclamation envoys as [generic] 'envoys?'" (安有世子敢稱詔使爲使臣乎). To sit across from the prince as though he were of the same status as the king and to endure the title "envoy" were demeaning and outrageous.

Despite Kim Allo's attempted refutations, Gong was adamant that the proposed ceremonial notes were insulting. If the Chosŏn court were to insist on the east-west arrangement, and presumably the "envoy" designation, Gong threatened, not only would neither he nor the assistant envoy would attend the banquet, they would cut short their stay in Seoul and return to Ming early. The only way to go through with the banquet, Gong told him, was to seat the envoys to the north, the crown prince to the east, and the king to west; this would correctly express the relative ranks of all involved in this particular context. Kim did not respond but rather forwarded to problem to the court for discussion.

King Chungjong was irritated as he asked the state councilors for their advice. First State Councilor Kim Kŭnsa 金謹思 advised the king to follow Gong's prescription, but could not do so without commenting that Gong was fussy and arrogant. Kim Allo and Third State Councilor (*uŭijŏng* 右議政) Yun Ŭnbo also agreed that there would be no harm in changing the seating arrangement and terminology to satisfy Gong's demands. The decision to redraft the ceremonial notes was not so much from a realization of the strength of Gong Yongqing's argument as it was a desire simply to avoid further confrontation. The stakes were potentially quite large should the hosting go poorly. The court was well aware of this and rather than push pedantic adherence to precedent, the king and state council were unanimous in giving Gong his way, despite Kim Kŭnsa's criticism of

Gong's character.

A regular feature of the envoys' time in Chosŏn was the negotiation of gifts. The Chosŏn court prepared an array of gifts that the envoys regularly refused, at least initially, in a performance of their supposed concern for the financial well-being of the Chosŏn king and country and their virtuous removal from material concerns as they represented their emperor abroad. It was often the case, however, that after initial refusals and a round or two of Chosŏn official pleading with them to accept the gifts, they often did. While the acceptance of gifts in and of itself was not really a problem, what irritated some members of the Chosŏn court was the way in which the envoys abandoned their feigned material disinterest.

The day after their arrival in Seoul, Second Royal Secretary (*chwasŭngji* 左承旨) Hwang Hŏn 黃憲 reported to the court his efforts to convince the envoys to accept the gifts King Chungjong had prepared for them.[131] As Hwang delivered the list of gifts to the envoys as they were going to bed, they both protested that it was too late and instructed Hwang to wait until morning. Undeterred, Hwang continued, acknowledging how perfect the envoys' virtue was in refusing to accept all gifts the king had offered on

131 Hwang Hŏn's report and the ensuing discussion between King Chungjong and the royal secretaries can be found in *Chungjong sillok* 32/3/11.

the road, but the king was increasingly unhappy that all his gifts had been refused. Gong Yongqing countered that all the food and lodging on the road had been a gift of the king and there was no way they could justify accepting even more. Hwang, pressed on, brushing off the room and board of the road as mere "local products" (*t'osan* 土産), not gifts from the king himself. Refusal of the king's gifts, Hwang, continued, would surely sadden the king to no end. It was at this point that Gong relented and conceded that if accepting the gifts were a matter of ritual propriety, it would be appropriate to accept them. He would not, however, accept them from Hwang, but only from the king personally at the following day's banquet.

Upon hearing Hwang's report, Pak Hongnin countered that the king giving gifts personally to the envoys at the banquet would be a violation of propriety. Fourth Royal Secretary (*chwabu sŭngji* 左副承旨) Kang Hyŏn 姜顯 noted that whenever Gong brought up ritual propriety (*ye* 禮) in the matter of gifts, it meant he wanted to accept them, suggesting that the appropriateness or inappropriateness of the king personally giving the gift was not a part of Gong's calculus. King Chungjong agreed with Kang that Gong wanted to accept the gifts. Gong invoked ritual propriety, the king opined, because he did not want to accept the gifts from his inferior, Hwang Hŏn. The king also agreed with Pak that while it was acceptable to give gifts directly to Japanese envoys at banquets, there was not precedent for doing so with Ming envoys. Despite the lack of precedent, Chungjong decided he would once more ask Gong at the banquet to accept the gifts; he wanted to find a way to enable Gong to accept the gifts while still maintaining some sense of decorum, as though he had to accept them only under pressure from the king. In effect, the king was looking for a path to Gong's accepting the gifts regardless of previous ritual precedent.

While not in opposition to the king, Pak Hongnin was not content to let the matter rest with the king's decision to ask Gong to accept the gifts at the banquet. While Wu Ximeng, the assistant envoy, was polite and humble, Pak conceded, Gong Yongqing was irritating and arrogant. He was rude at the previous banquet in refusing wine and being visibly insincere in offering wine to the king. His refusal to accept gifts that he clearly wanted was only further evidence of his general insincerity. After concluding this litany, however, Pak agreed that there would be no harm in the king personally asking Gong to accept the gifts.

The king decided to ask Gong to accept the gifts once and then see how he reacted so as to try to gauge whether or not to push harder or accept his refusal as sincere. This approach worried Kang Hyŏn who warned the king that Gong was in essence a shallow flake. There was no use playing subtle language games with him and, moreover, it would be unlikely the interpreters would be able to convey the subtly such soundings of Gong's intentions would require. Better to say as little as possible, as simply as possible, so as to reduce the possibility of misinterpretation. For Kang, this danger far outweighed any benefit that might be accrued in furtive attempts to cajole Gong into accepting the gifts he obviously wanted, as though it was only to satisfy the fragile emotions of the king.

The Chosŏn court consensus was that Gong Yongqing was a transparently simplistic man of base motivation and patent insincerity. And yet, the king and his court were mobilized to ensure his happiness. Was there enough wine? Were there enough fruit plates? How could he be made to accept the gifts that everyone knew he wanted? Pak and Kang were blunt in their assessments of Gong's qualities, but the king did not respond to them. His only interests were in the fact that Gong had revealed, perhaps inadvertently, perhaps purposely, his desires, and in how he might be able to satisfy them. The task at hand was to ensure the complete satisfaction of the envoys during their time in Chosŏn.

The most taxing of the challenges of hosting the envoys was the question of personal behavior. Their stay in Seoul was marred by a noted lack of restraint ranging from ignoring minor social graces to simply foul recklessness. At one banquet, Gong Yongqing encouraged the assembly to drink to excess, while he himself drank little. The result was that some, like Minister of Rites Yun In'gyŏng 尹仁鏡, drank themselves sick. Capital Magistrate (*p'anyun* 判尹) O Kyŏl 吳潔 was so drunk that he fell off his horse as he tried to leave and eventually had to be sent home in a palanquin. Gong, however, remained sober, all the while making disparaging jokes about the Chosŏn officials in attendance. In reference to Kim Allo, who had protested Gong's outrage at the ceremonial notes for the crown prince banquet, he asked, "How many concubines does the second state councilor have?" (左相有妾幾人). Answering his own question, Gong said, "The second state councilor is afraid of his wife, so he definitely cannot stable any concubines" (左相畏內室想必不畜). He asked how many concubines Reception Envoy Chŏng Saryong had and again answered himself, "I think this man has three" (此人想有妾三人). He pointed to Yun In'gyŏng, the Chosŏn minister of rites, and said, "This is a man who has a concubine but no children from his wife" (此人有妾而於正室無子者也).[132]

While the tasteless jokes at the expense of high officials drunk to the point of incapacitation was bad enough, the worst behavior was at the

132 For Hwang Hŏn's complete report to the king on this party, see *Chungjong sillok* 32/3/17.

banquet for the envoys at Kyŏnghoe-ru, the great raised pavilion on the grounds of the royal palace.[133] The envoys arrived in the early afternoon and immediately began to depart from expected behavior. They wanted to change into informal clothing for the banquet and invited the king to do the same. He refused. The envoys later repeated their intention to change into casual clothing and again invited the king to do the same. And again, the king refused. The envoys went ahead and changed into casual clothing, much to the chagrin of the king's entourage. The entry in the *Veritable Records* notes that their refusal to wear appropriate attire was an irritation to all and finally made everyone in attendance aware that the envoys were fundamentally frivolous and inappropriate (侍臣無不憤恨始知其輕薄不中也).

The banquet was not planned to take place on the upper deck of the pavilion, but the envoys wanted to go up to see the view. The king readily assented. Once on the upper deck, the envoys commented on the commanding view. The envoys, in all likelihood, Gong Yongqing, commented on the location of Kyŏnghoe-ru in relation to Paegak Mountain, "This pavilion is truly marvelous, but it would really be good if the position of that mountain [Paegak] was a little to the east. I comment

---

133 The complete account of the banquet, the envoys' behavior, and the ensuing discussions between King Chungjong and his court are to be found in *Chungjong sillok* 32/3/14.

on this because my knowledge of geomancy is quite thorough" (此樓最妙但彼山{白岳也}之座稍東則甚好我粗知風水故語及於此也). The king, taking their poor behavior in stride, and well aware of their fondness of renaming Chosŏn built and natural landscapes, invited the envoys to rename the principle mountains surrounding the capital, which they readily did, despite their unsatisfactory locations.

A little later, the king and the envoys descended from the pavilion and, at the envoys' insistence, walked in the flower gardens below. The envoys mused that the beautiful flowers of the royal gardens were well-suited to adorn the heads of elders but, being too young, they could not wear them. The king replied that as the envoys were young and beautiful, the flowers were upset at not adorning their heads. Delighted, the envoys picked some camellia blossoms and affixed them haphazardly to the right and left sides of their caps, and then asked the king to do the same. The king commanded a servant to fetch a single flower, which he pushed into his winged cap though a hole on the left side. Not yet content, the envoys wanted the king to place two flowers in his cap, as they had done, but the king's cap had only one hole on the left. Instead, he had to run the flower stem through an eyelet in the strap of his cap. The envoys were pleased and praised him in childish tones. This sort of behavior went on throughout the walk through the gardens, causing continual humiliation to the king and his entourage. And yet, as the *Veritable Records* compiler noted in this entry, the king maintained his composure throughout, enduring every slight with grace.

The repeated embarrassments of the afternoon culminated in the evening near the end of the banquet. Gong Yongqing called for a table to set up for him to write some calligraphy. He had his interpreter from Liaodong, Kang Zhen 康鎮, arrange two young *kisaeng* courtesans to hold candles at either side of the desk and four more to dance before him as he wrote. Gong instructed the Kang that the two *kisaeng* holding candles be of the same height and, wanting to better see the face of one of them, told her to move the flower ornaments in her hair. As he moved his brush to write, rather than touch the brush to the paper, he flicked it as to splatter ink across her face and clothing. He did this repeatedly as he taunted her, his desire evidently overriding any sense of self-restraint he might have had. The Chosŏn ministers sat stunned and uncomprehending.[134]

Many remonstrated with the king to end Gong's atrocious behavior. Inspector-General (*taesahŏn* 大司憲) Kwŏn Ye 權輗 pleaded with the king,

134 For an additional account of this incident, see Wang, *Boundless Winds of Empire*, 227-9.

noting that the envoys' behavior had been unacceptable throughout the afternoon and into the evening. The king's tolerance, Kwŏn noted, was admirable, but there were limits:

> Your Majesty serves the great with perfect sincerity and so hosts the imperial envoys, obeying their every request. Although this is so, the conduct of a lord of others cannot be like this. Even though [you] serve the great with perfect sincerity and host the celestial envoys with perfect respect, with this violation of propriety, how can one speak of sincerity or respect?
>
> 殿下事大至誠故接待華使一從其請然人君擧止不可如是事大雖以誠也待天使雖致敬也豈可失禮而曰以誠以敬哉[135]

Kwŏn crossed something of a boundary in this statement. In contrasting the sincerity and respect of the king with the gross violations of the chief envoy, he framed the ritual practices in the royal hosting of the imperial envoy as representations of actual sentiment. Moreover, the authentic sentiment is betrayed by the coarse and brutish behavior of the envoy wholly unaware of the royal earnestness. Employing the terms of

135 *Chungjong sillok* 32/3/14.

the *sadae chaso* relationship, how can one be sincere and respectful in this situation? How can the small Chosŏn serve the great Ming when the great Ming will not nurture the small Chosŏn? The mutual obligations collapse in Kwŏn's formulation when one party refuses to play its role. How can the king perform his duties when his Ming counterpart refuses to perform his at every turn, with every gesture, every breath? Why should the king continue to submit himself and his court to this humiliation?

King Chungjong responded to his officials with a combination of understanding and frustration. He readily agreed that the events of the day and that very evening were unacceptable in the extreme, but he refused to react in such a way as to cause offence to the envoys. It was not out of some misguided sense of sincerity or respect, as Kwŏn Ye had suggested. Rather, the king had a particular policy objective in mind, one that might well be derailed if he or his court mishandled the situation. In responding to Kwŏn's calling for the king to confront the envoys, King Chungjong replied,

> The genealogy issue is of exceeding importance and we have already asked [the envoys] about it. If the envoys return happy, then we might succeed, but if they return angry, how could it not be the beginning of a crisis?

宗系之事甚重而旣已請之矣兩使各喜悅而還則可以成之若
慍怒而還則豈不爲生事乎[136]

The genealogy issue refers to the way in which several official Ming texts, notably the *Collected Statutes of the Great Ming* (*Da ming huidian* 大明會典), recorded the founding of the Chosŏn state. Among other issues, these texts identified Yi Sŏnggye 李成桂, first king of the Chosŏn dynasty, as the son of Yi Inim 李仁任, Yi Sŏnggye's notorious rival and, in fact, no relation, despite the shared surname. This idea had been planted in the Ming court by Koryŏ loyalists Yun I 尹彛 and Yi Ch'o 李初 in order to besmirch the legitimacy of Yi Sŏnggye and new Chosŏn state. The Chosŏn court became aware of this problem in 1394 and asked the Ming court repeatedly to correct the error, but despite repeated Ming promises to do so, nearly 200 years passed before the correction finally made it to print and arrived in Chosŏn in 1589.[137]

King Chungjong mentioned the genealogy problem to the envoys on several occasions during their stay in Seoul. Since the issue gnawed

---

136 *Chungjong sillok* 32/3/14.

137 Ŏ Sukkwŏn, "P'aegwan chapki," 117-8; Ŏ Sukkwŏn, *Storyteller's Miscellany*, 71-4; Sŏ Munjung, *Choya kimun* (Sŏngnam: Han'gukhak Chŏngsin Munhwa Yon'guwŏn, 2000), 73-6; Yi Kŭngik, *Kugyŏk yŏllyŏsil kisul IV*, trans. Yi Irhae and Yi Sik (Sŏul: Minjok Munhwa Ch'ujinhoe, 1985), 363-371, 768-771; Wang, *Boundless Winds of Empire*, 160-6.

at successive Chosŏn kings, this is not surprising, but there was a special urgency in this particular instance because it came to the king's attention that Gong Yongqing was on the revision committee for the next edition of the *Collected Statutes*. After many failed attempts to move the Ming government to make the editorial changes, Gong's presence seemed like an especially fortuitous event and an opportunity not to be wasted.[138] Just before the envoys were to leave Seoul, the king reiterated to the Royal Secretariat the importance of treating the envoys well and sending them home happy:

> During the fireworks display at Kyŏnghoe-ru, the envoys said that every explosion was beautiful and added, "Were it not for you, worthy king, how would we be able to see such a splendid event?" These words expressed their enjoyment. The envoys have now heard about revising the genealogy and they say, "There is nothing more important than this. When we return to court we will work hard for this." We must make an extra effort in hosting them so that they are pleased. If there is a martial arts demonstration at Mohwa-gwan tomorrow as additional entertainment for their pleasure, the celestial envoys will certainly depart happy and say upon their return, "Chosŏn treated us extremely well" and thereafter work hard

138 *Chungjong sillok* 32/3/13.

to help in revising the genealogy.

慶會樓觀火時天使於每火稱美且云若非賢王何以得見此盛事乎云此喜之之言也改宗系事天使聞之乃曰此莫大之事也俺等還朝廷當力爲之云須當別致厚待之意使之歡喜可也明日餞宴設武藝於慕華館以助別程之歡則天使必極歡而還曰朝鮮待俺等甚厚云而其於改宗系亦必力助之矣[139]

King Chungjong could not have been more clear. The envoys must be pleased with their journey so that they will exert themselves in the revision of the *Collected Statutes* on behalf of Chosŏn. It was a neither a matter of sincerity nor of respect, contrary to Kwŏn Ye's protestations. And it most certainly was not related to the personal behavior of the envoys. There was a policy objective to be secured and ensuring the envoys' pleasure was, at least in Chungjong's thinking, the surest way to do so.

There are a number of possible explanations for Chungjong's concern with this matter. It is arguable that he was concerned about the legitimacy of the dynasty. He may have been concerned about his own legitimacy. Yi Sŏnggye had come to power through a coup, as indeed Chungjong himself had, minor though he was. Sixiang Wang has argued, however, that

139 *Chungjong sillok* 32/3/16.

these were not Chungjong's concerns with the genealogy issue. Successive Ming emperors had already granted investiture to successive Chosŏn kings and Chungjong himself already had Ming investiture so his own position was secure. What was at stake was the continued *sadae chaso* mythology. A Chosŏn state born of a coup d'état by the son of a court official did not fit the moral narrative of the Chosŏn-Ming relationship in which the small Chosŏn served the great Ming with sincerity and respect. It is this narrative that provided the space for Chosŏn diplomatic agency in an otherwise grossly asymmetrical relationship. As long as Chosŏn played its role, it could demand the same of Ming.[140]

The juxtaposition of the missing entries of *Travel Log of the Celestial Envoys* with the richness and complexity of the entries in the *Veritable Records* throws the simplicity of the *Travel Log* into sharp relief. The indignities suffered by the Chosŏn king and court are a jolting contrast to the relatively smooth experiences of Reception Envoy Chŏng Saryong as he traveled with the envoys. It is in this differentiation that a proper reading of the *Travel Log* emerges. Chungjong and his court were mobilized to seize an opportunity to present the case for correcting the Chosŏn

140 Wang, *Boundless Winds of Empire*, 165-6.

royal genealogy in the *Collected Statutes of the Great Ming* to a Ming official directly involved in the editing process. The exchange between Chungjong and Kwŏn Ye shows that the king's approach was in no way related to an authentic sincerity in serving the great or to respecting envoys utterly unworthy of respect. Rather, he was engaged in maintaining the operation of a tributary discourse that opened spaces for Chosŏn diplomatic agency. And as his injunctions to Kwŏn and to the Royal Secretariat make clear, the primary tactic in this larger strategy was treating the Ming envoys well, whether they were deserving or not.

As it elides the worst of Gong Yongqing's transgressions while at the same time omitting the lapses on the parts of the Royal Cuisine Office and the Reception Commission, we might best consider the *Travel Log* a tactical text. It is not an objective record of events, but rather a selective narrative of making envoys happy, a critically important part of a larger campaign to influence the Ming understanding of the Chosŏn founding, which in turn, was central to the smooth operation of the Chosŏn-Ming tributary discourse, and ultimately to the preservation of Chosŏn diplomatic agency in a severely asymmetrical relationship.

Bibliography

Becker, Carl. *The Heavenly City of the Eighteenth-Century Philosophers*. New Haven: Yale University Press, 1932.

Chŏng Saryong 정사룡 et al. comp. *Ch'ŏnsa illo ilgi: Chosŏn, myŏng nara sasin ŭl matta* 천사일로일기: 조선, 명나라 사신을 맞다. Translated by Kim Yunjo, Yi Chian, and Hwang Tonggwŏn. Taegu: Kyemyŏng Taehakkyo Ch'ulp'anbu, 2020.

Chungjong sillok 中宗實錄 https://sillok.history.go.kr/main/main.do

Deng Lin 鄧林 ed. *Xinchu jingjiao sishu buzhu beizhi* 新出精校四書補註備旨. Shanghai: Tianbao Shuju, 1916.

Feng Lihua 馮李驊 and Lu Hao 陸浩 eds. *Jingjiao zuo xiu* 精校左繡. Shanghai: Huiwentang, 1911.

Hucker, Charles. *A Dictionary of Official Titles in Imperial China*. Stanford: Stanford University Press, 1985.

Hwanghwa chip 皇華集. Sŏul: Ch'ŏngun Munhwasa, 1994.

Iryŏn 一然. *Chŭngbo samguk yusa* 增補三國遺事. Sŏul: Minjung Sŏgwan, 1954.

"Jiongzhuo" 泂酌 in *Shijing beizhi* 詩經備旨. Edited by Zou Shengmai 鄒聖脉. Shanghai: Wensheng Shuju, 1904.

Kang Boseong. "Land Reform in the Realization of a Confucian Ideal: The Debate among Neo-Confucian Scholars in the Mid-Chosŏn Period." *Acta Koreana* 25, no. 2 (December 2022): 1-18.

Kim Chŏngho 金正浩. *Taedong chiji* 大東地志. Sŏul: Hanyang Taehakkyo Pusŏl Kukhak Yŏn'guwŏn, 1974.

Kim Pusik 金富軾. *Samguk sagi* 三國史記. Sŏul: Minjok Munhwa Ch'ujinhoe, 1973.

Kim Pusik. "Kŏsŏgan Hyŏkkŏse" in *The Silla Annals of the Samguk Sagi*. Translated by Kenneth H. J. Gardiner et al. Seongnam, Korea: The Academy of Korean Studies Press, 2013.

Kim Pusik. "Sage King Tongmyŏng" in *The Koguryŏ Annals of the Samguk Sagi*. Translated by Kenneth H. J. Gardiner et al. Seongnam, Korea: The Academy of Korean Studies Press, 2011.

Kim Yunjo 김윤조, "Ch'ŏnsa illo ilgi haeje" 천사일로일기 해제 in Chŏng Saryong et al. comp., *Ch'ŏnsa illo ilgi: Chosŏn, myŏng nara sasin ŭl matta* 천사일로일기: 조선, 명 나라 사신을 맞다. Translated by Kim Yunjo 김윤조, Yi Chian 이지안, and Hwang Tonggwŏn 황동권. Taegu: Kyemyŏng Taehakkyo Ch'ulp'anbu, 2020.

Kong Yonggyŏng 龔用卿. *Sa chosŏn rok* 使朝鮮錄. Sŏul: Han'guk Kojŏn Kanhaenghoe, 1975.

Namgung Chun 南宮濬, ed. *Sŏjŏn ku t'ohae* 書傳具吐解. Kyŏngsŏng: Yuil Sŏgwan, 1912.

"Nanshan you tai" 南山有臺 in *Shijing beizhi* 詩經備旨. Edited by Zou Shengmai 鄒聖脉. Shanghai: Wensheng Shuju, 1904.

No Sasin 盧思愼 et al. comp. *Sinjŭng tongguk yŏji sŭngnam* 新增東國輿地勝覽.

Sŏul: Myŏngmundang, 1994.

O Hŭibok 오희복. *Kwallyo kigu mit kwanjingmyŏng p'yŏllam* 관료기구 및 관직명 편람. Sŏul: Yŏgang, 1999.

Ŏ Sukkwŏn 魚叔權. "P'aegwan chapki" 稗官雜記 in *Taedong yasŭng* 大東野乘, vol. 1. Sŏul: Kyŏnghŭi Ch'ulp'ansa, 1968.

Ŏ Sukkwŏn. *A Korean Storyteller's Miscellany*. Translated by Peter H. Lee. Princeton: Princeton University Press, 1989.

Pak Yongdae 朴容大 et al. comp. *Chŭngbo munhŏn pigo* 增補文獻備考. Sŏul: Tongguk Munhwasa, 1959.

Palais, James. *Confucian Statecraft and Korean Institutions: Yu Hyŏngwŏn and the Late Chosŏn Dynasty*. Seattle: University of Washington Press, 1996.

"Sanghu" 桑扈 in *Shijing beizhi* 詩經備旨. Edited by Zou Shengmai 鄒聖脉. Shanghai: Wensheng Shuju, 1904.

"Shu er" 述而 in *Xinchu jingjiao sishu buzhu beizhi* 新出精校四書補註備旨. Edited by Deng Lin 鄧林. Shanghai: Tianbao Shuju, 1916.

Sim Paekchun 심백준 and Tam Ryangso 담량소. *Samguk chi sajŏn* 三國志事典. Translated by Chŏng Wŏn'gi 정원기. Sŏul: Pŏmusa, 2000.

Sŏ Munjung 徐文重. *Choya kimun* 朝野記聞. Sŏngnam: Han'guk Chŏngsin Munhwa Yon'guwŏn, 2000.

Tongguk yŏji pigo 東國輿地備攷. Sŏul: Sŏul T'ŭkpyŏlsisa P'yŏnch'an Wiwŏnhoe, 1956.

Tongyanghak Yŏn'guso 東洋學研究所, comp. *Han'guk hanchaŏ sajŏn* 韓國漢字語辭典. Sŏul: Tan'guk Taehakkyo Ch'ulp'anbu, 1997.

Van Lieu, Joshua. "Chosŏn-Qing Tributary Discourse: Transgression, Restoration, and Textual Performativity." *Cross-Currents: East Asian History and Culture*

Review 7, no. 2 (2018): 326-363.

Wagner, Edward Willett. *The Literati Purges: Political Conflict in Early Yi Korea.* Cambridge: Harvard University Press, 1974.

Wang, Sixiang. *Boundless Winds of Empire: Rhetoric and Ritual in Early Chosŏn Diplomacy with Ming China.* New York: Columbia University Press, 2023.

Xue Zhongsan 薛仲三 and Ouyang Yi 歐陽頤. *Liang qian nian zhong xi li dui zhao biao* 兩千年中西曆對照表. Taibei: Guomin Chubanshe, 1958.

Yi Hŭisŭng 李熙昇 et al. *Han'guk inmyŏng tae sajŏn* 韓國人名大事典. Sŏul: Sin'gu Munhwasa, 1967.

Yi Kŭngik 李肯翊. *Kugyŏk yŏllyŏsil kisul IV* 국역 연려실기술 IV. Translated by Yi Irhae 이일해 and Yi Sik 이식. Sŏul: Minjok Munhwa Ch'ujinhoe, 1985.

Yi Nŭnghwa 李能和. *Han'guk togyo sa* 韓國道教史. Sŏul: Tongguk Taehakkyo, 1959.

Yŏnsan-gun ilgi 燕山君日記 https://sillok.history.go.kr/main/main.do

Yu Mongin 유몽인. *Ŏu yadam* 어우야담. Translated by Sin Ikch'ŏl, Yi Hyŏngdae, Cho Yunghŭi, and No Yŏngmi. Sŏul: Tolbegae, 2022.

Yu Mongin 유몽인. *Ŏu yadam: wŏnmun* 於于野談: 원문. Sŏul: Tolbegae, 2019.

"Zhongyong" 中庸 in *Xinchu jingjiao sishu buzhu beizhi* 新出精校四書補註備旨. Edited by Deng Lin 鄧林. Shanghai: Tianbao Shuju, 1916.

Zou Shengmai 鄒聖脉, ed. *Shujing beizhi* 書經備旨. n.p.: 1886.

Zou Shengmai 鄒聖脉, ed. *Shujing beizhi* 書經備旨. Shanghai: Huiwentang Shuju, 1904.

Zuo Tradition. Translated by Stephen Durant, Wai-yee Li, and David Schaburg. Seattle: University of Washington Press, 2016.

Index

A

B

C

D

E

F

G

H

I

J

K

L

M

N

O

P

Q

R

S

T

U

V

W

X

Y

Z

About the translator

Joshua Van Lieu is a historian of early modern and modern East Asian politics, thought, and critical international relations. He received his doctoral degree from the University of Washington in the histories of Chosŏn Korea and Late Imperial China. He has published on nineteenth-century Qing-Chosŏn tribute politics, the historiography of reform movements in late Chosŏn Korea, the political roles of the Chosŏn state Guanti cult, and on critical approaches to historical international relations. He is currently an associate professor in the Department of History at Keimyung University.

About the editor

Lee Jonghan is a professor in the Department of Chinese and Chinese Studies, College of Humanities and International Studies, Keimyung University and Director of Dongsan Library. He is interested in the study of Chinese prose, including the works of Han Yu, as well as the translation of Chinese classics. His publications include *The Prose Works of Hanyu: A Korean Translation with Annotations* (5 volumes, selected as an outstanding publication by the Korean Academy of Sciences in 2013).

About Keimyung University Dongsan Library

Keimyung University Dongsan Library has over 78,000 old books, including 23 types and 97 volumes of State-designated Treasures such as *Yongbi ŏch'ŏn ka* (Songs of flying dragons) and 8 types and 18 volumes of Daegu City Tangible Cultural Property such as *Taegu ŭpchi* (Daegu county gazetteer). As one of Korea's representative institutions housing an extensive collection of old books, Dongsan Library contributes to the systematic management of Korea's traditional cultural heritage and the promotion of Korean studies research by holding exhibitions as well as publishing catalogs, annotated texts and translations.

Source Text:
Ch'ŏnsa illo ilgi

迎于江滸兩使招摠兵官上舡判書與從事官及通事等行拜
禮訖率一行人先下船拱立岸前兩使與摠兵官步就岸上判書
與一行人就前再拜兩使答揖遂告辭還就舟中兩使入摠兵官
宴廳使頭目高嵩康鎮等追謂伴送使曰宜即過江我等當於此
望見判書還歸而去是日過江時兩使家人等請轎子所設朱簾
及豹皮依即給之兩使稱謝前日宴中贈給馬匹兩使到江上揮
手使之牽還回舟泊於江邊仍坐船上是時日已下舂兩使還於宴
廳外起立向北遙揖伴送使等亦擧手應之竢兩使發行乃
還禮曹所送高嵩等處人情物件令義州官收藏待謝 恩使
行次寄送于遼東

後兩使別酌一盃遍屬遠接使及從事官平安都事義州牧使[illegible]
令撥宴李希輔朴守良告辭而退兩使即乘轎伴送使李一行
追到鴨綠江船上設卓子巡酒數杯兩使顧聘乘渡出言曰
際或不能成言上使尤有慘色令譯官謂伴送使曰後日貢使
之來輒須寄書我若因公事出外則吳老必在京吳老若出
則我必在京遂揮涕不已於是伴送使及一行人馬等下至僕
隸亦皆下淚伴送使與從事官以次進酒畢兩使畫指一行
之人饋酒且謂伴送使曰 殿下上爲 朝廷盡誠下爲
我等盡情我等還朝何敢一日忘于懷每頭君將此意
之意另 啓于 殿下 身至北岸 摠兵官李景良來

送云李希輔朴守良等各次二三篇仍叙別懷以呈上使謂譯官曰
汝國之士何皆能文耶於此便知人才之盛矣又問曰都監官獨
不作詩何也答曰雖是文官不解製述故不敢作也兩使相顧曰一
何謹慎如此乎○兩使作留別詩各送于遠接使及餞慰使陪事
官等處○副使送星槎勝覽及夏言所著郊祀奏議時政奏議
等冊于遠接使曰星槎勝覽則只有一本須於今夜謄書追送原
本于湯站

初八日晴浪時兩使坐大廳招遠接使及餞慰使共飲飲已即發行至江上
宴廳出所製長留別詩篇分贈一行人員及一路守令等又各將手
簡付承旨使 啓于 上兩使各就坐遠接使餞慰使各行酒

各行酒初昏罷宴李希輔朴守良就兩使前告辭兩使曰不欲送我於江上耶且欲致簡於 殿下俟後日更來稟也○是日天使所求大小硯各一面令李和宗等呈給兩使前日有 命所載中硯時未刻造故不得贈與

初六日晴在義州遠接使送金綠鳳各一部于兩使蓋前日在碧蹄驛時來請故也兩使曰前偶戲言果不忘也各取三枝曰只此足矣兩使謂譯官曰我等驅馳之餘心神俱疲欲又留歇一箇日判書必不催我行也今日宴席且須休設

初七日雨在義州午後行留日宴兩使出坐遠接使等各行酒畢○上使出途中所作詩十餘篇送于遠接使仍令餞慰使等皆和

雜之事曰同雜所以雜此者盖由彼此人民密邇居住潛相往來故也
兩使答曰許多事情今已細悉矣遠接起辭退上使就執遠接使之手
曰一別之後判書無由見我我亦何從見判書乎念及於此不覺令人
惨然令通事洪謙呈 殿試策登科榜目于兩使兩使
覽訖曰多謝 殿下遠意但何只此兩策乎洪謙答曰舉一
可知其三矣上使曰汝能讀書人也○午都司迎慰使趙仁奎往
黔同島設迎慰宴而來○夕設餞慰宴于大廳上使出坐遠接使
與餞慰使李希輔別餞慰使朴守良等入行禮各就坐遠接
使令譯官告曰都司迎慰使趙仁奎來在此兩使呼使預宴令遼
東來優人等作雜戲於中 朴擧旨先進餞慰盃後遠接使以下

嘴說湯站指揮而去圖成來此即送于湯站使之轉送于遼東韋其已
是白我方從朝鮮賦來就回到北京當開刊印出付提督主事轉送
貴國云云辰時兩使出大聽招遠撫使共飯後仍就兩使前說夾江事之
首尾兩使答曰我等在朝時已詳聞此事及有此行楊御史行中
謂夾江之事實關事體須要分別疆界各守法度於我性年巡
按遼東時當定奪此事云云我等行到遼陽史御史亦道此事如
楊御史之言又屬寧都御史謂我等曰朝鮮 國王啟事
朝廷凡有走回人口皆厚給般盟纏解送于此愈恩久不怠甚賢可嘉若
不褒聞儀將獎則何以勸人之善云云今次我等之回當更說遼東屬
寧等御史將夾江禁耕之事著為成法遠撫使又言往時金同

初四日晴兩使出坐大廳遠接使入行禮仍呈水獺皮單字兩使相與耳語
仍答曰我等已領 殿下愛敬之誠不令須說也覩面既不當受況此物
乎判書與我等同行日久豈不知我等心事乎即令揮手取去
遠接使再三固請竟不聽早食後兩使發行到良策館晝點過
古津江取儒子坐於石橋觀水至所串點心申時到義順館令退行餞慰宴乎
明日○遼東御史差送伶人十四名到此待候又揔兵官李景良領
軍一千五百名來到安州堡差千戶二人揔旗四名問安于兩使
初五日晴在義順館上使令譯官語于遠接使曰我等驅馳道路
勞勩殊甚欲留兩三日初七八日間過江但勤殿宴會畫
國王曾許繪送而何至今不來耶若於過江前不及來則我等當

氣凡海味遇南風即臭腐不可食且害人蝦房烹之有妙法前是
妙法外此有帶殼煮食有帶殼蒸食者有取其肉而和以糯煎而
食者皆妙此海中之上品不可不知上使又手寫示曰判書若有閑我
未嘗不以實告正見斯文一氣之雅何嫌何疑乎又云行步之禮出以闑
東爲左入以闑西爲左可不不仔細看

初三日晴卯時兩使出坐大廳遠接使入行禮今日路長行忙輒停宴禮
可也遂發行至雲興館畫點又到林畔點上畫方飯兩使問判書
曰安在即欲共飯譯官對曰判書不知老爹有命在下處曾已
飯矣兩使曰退了三四日便當分袂今後例於安歇之處輒令共飯
乘昏至車輦館令停宿所宴

亦數十不同年不同月不同日不同時生者不待論而知其間亦有同月同日
而生者有同時而生者何以辨之因此以生時之先後為鴈行之次第以鴈行之
次第定兄弟之長幼輪定次序毫髮不差一相聚間不須問年齒
而可知長幼也皆自一起或輪至千至百至數十皆倣此杜詩所謂高
三年五許十二雀十九正謂此也祖則有祖之等輩父則有父之等輩子
則有子行之等輩不相凌犯中庸謂燕毛所以序齒亦此意上使又小錄
一紙曰烹蟹房之法切不可去其本來之汁若別以水澆之即無味矣
其法多用豚油熬令滾而蟹房投之用筯攪之量其將熟或用酒
或用糯湯小許和之雖用糯湯亦須用酒方去腥氣亦不可太過亦不可
不及量其得宜即可食矣凡滋味烹之皆須用酒雖小亦可方去腥

初二日晴辰時兩使坐齋山亭遠接使觀察使兩行禮畢觀察使告辭而出兩使發行至納清亭招遠接使共晝飯令譯官語曰 勤政殿宴享之時我等請 殿下曰佳會云難又請晝宴會畱見贈 殿下許之而至今不來判書督我須速啓爲遠接使答曰路遠行迫恐不能及然則須付湯站指揮韓承慶令轉送于遼東我等當說與承慶而去兩使令射官等射帿謂遠接使曰判書家人徐壽千龍泉郡守曹世鳳射藝絶倫可稟知於 殿下夕至定州令退行宿所宴於明朝上使頭目一人怒其房守人因拳毆又一人以驛隷失其笠冒逼令備納上使聞之即拿頭目等數其罪而杖之上使錄小紙以示曰所云數十八者即是鴈行之序今 中國大族兄弟輩多至數千次亦數百次

又告成賓人家喜種松與梅竹土人以常暖故不着襦衣我等仕後不得做
御唄有祖父孝服斬之許遂翻服闋還京僅四介月又欽差以來有此
在堂兄弟共五人伯氏早歿其餘皆秀才云兩使又論古今詩集乃
曰中朝文士喜讀李杜元白詩云午後兩使渡慱川江登控江亭
招遠樓觀察等使共飯仍設小酌兩使見亭上所題懸板此何人所
寫乎極有楷法答曰乃隨我來人柳耳孫之筆也兩使亟招耳孫給
與魚肉曰曾見汝面而已未知汝有寫才也兩使見嘉山路左有石
獨立引轎下立良久摩挲之至嘉山設宿所宴于齊山亭高巖
兩使招射官等射帳安州房守人向壽千上使自安州帶來于此
使諭大學而聽之

潦 興

文献通考事文類聚等冊乎遠接使答曰皆有之但文苑英華只有高麗時舊本殘缺居多 殿下近欲印出廣布中外令朝貢使臣求買於 中朝今年始得寫本以來亦有鋟文 京師官本果為稀罕耶兩使答曰此書乃宋朝人所撰合一百卷 中國亦難得今本權等家亦無此冊曾聞有人用銀十五兩收買於雲南人以謂賤買 國王苟欲見之何不奏請今本乎遠接使問潮汐之理上使曰氣使之然也於人若呼吸遠接使曰東海無潮何也東方地側水傍所鍾如盃盂盈滿所以無潮遠接使問副使曰常州罨畫溪罨字何義副使曰罨興掩同遠接使問上使曰福建風土何如福州在大海濱人家皆在高處平地則水居其半氣候常暖四時恒有名花

家令君只要三四日之程念及家宅者何耶必須送我於嘉山然後
方放公去也觀察使曰適有地方應　啓達公事故欲去今聞
尊命敢不敬承兩使發行至清川江乘樓船招遠接觀察兩使
共坐設酌從容談話因問　本國箕子以下建國世系遠接使令譯
官略道其大槩上使顧謂副使曰所謂三國興廢我詳考之矣因
歷舉朱蒙溫祚赫居世始起之事甚詳且謂譯官曰此等事跡
流入中國載在諸史故我知其顛末如此又曰吾鄉人謗傳高麗始
祖王建乃福州長樂縣人子孫相傳為王五百年且安南國主陳氏亦
福建人也又曰汝　國追祀王建乎答曰於麻田郡立崇義殿春
享祀兩使曰此是美意又曰　貴國有史記漢書三國志晉書隋書唐書

四月

初一日晴辰時兩使坐大廳共飯遠接使觀察使入行禮仍告副使曰不能戒戢下人至於偷竊大人之硯惶恐惶恐副使笑曰此細事也何煩告我吾帶來之人不謹看守罪自有歸況紛擾之中不知何人之所偷今遽指摘人尤非所宜使此人被黯黮之罪竟陷偷竊之名則事之不祥莫此爲甚判書必欲馳　啓于　殿下我豈能安於心乎路上賦詩談謔之事亦當不爲也餞慰使告辭兩使各製詩一篇使　啓於

殿下又各賦詩贈別餞慰使及觀察使舊例平安道觀察使陪送

天使至於安州故觀察使李龜齡告辭於兩使兩使戲答曰黃海

觀察使送至境上獨奈何欲徑歸耶我輩萬里來使尚不敢恨

論仍及宦者事兩使問　本國宦者始宦之由李和宗等答曰本國不用宮刑民家生子若一家人因事俱出則兒在襁褓遺矢滿体狗從而舐之仍囓截陽莖而食凡　本國之宦者皆如此兩使不信以謂誑說問於遠接使等遠接等答曰亦如和宗等之言且謂曰　本國宦者之任　中朝為太監者張欽金義陳浩等亦如是矣此事彼輩之所詳知也兩使始信之曰　中國之宦者異於是焉凡罪人之子當隨坐者年不滿則械其死而宮之宦者之多以此故也又所謂張欽太監者善寫字有幹能　朝廷信任之云日沒設炬火於江岸影到江底見之若金柱然兩使倚楹而立招遠接使共觀嗟歎慨而罷

昨夜取燭之人十分無禮令已究問發遣遠驛分徒役完日亦當
馳 啓于 殿下矣上使曰答罰已重矣愼勿煩 啓辰時行宿
所宴于大廳副使頭目云老爹今朝出行李所帶硯面寫字
之後仍置案上未及收藏有不知多名房守人再三撫玩因而偷
去云云遠接使令拿致可疑者陽德房守人轉付觀察使使之窮
推兩使發行至雲巖院捨遠接及觀察使共飯巡酒數杯而罷
未時至安州設餞慰宴于百祥樓兩使乘轎到樓遠接及
觀察使餞慰使鄭百朋等各以次行禮兩使以坐勢背江命
移其座於南遠接等於東隅開宴奏女樂餞慰使先進盃訖
遠接等又各進酒夕兩使就檻前與遠接等相對平坐從容談

闡

之盛山川之秀儀從之蕆幷見之矣顧不穀匪人何幸入畫中圖也
他日幽齋高獨對景興思不盡東望之繾綣矣許參判敏行
迫草達　謝惟原亮兩使發行至斧山院柗遠接及觀察使
小酌而罷又至順安晝點副使所用京來硯匣房守人責持待
副使如廁頭目錢循欲奪取不與即強取擲地破壞無餘遠接使
問之令改造他匣午後兩使踰於波嶺安州等官人設帳幕於路
西高丘欲進茶果兩使不入夕至肅川令退行宿所宴于明朝上使
夜坐東軒燃燭寫詩官奴權孫再三上軒欲取燭跋呵禁不聽
上使怒拿送於遠接及觀察使等即令囚禁
二十九日晴遠接與觀察使同坐將權孫杖八十下使李和宗告上使曰

閱閒而國中山川文物盡在目中歷歷可覩真足為傳家之寶矣

不盡之感豈能云喻許參判回遼略申　謝忱亮之幸幸副使

簡曰不穀行次黃州辱　國王遣陪臣致宴生陽館來次平壤

僅百里復辱　國王遣吏曹許參判致宴參判才人之裔也進退諂度館

伴鄭判書禮文頻給久而益隆李觀察使設玩布奇懇邀獵

景艷判書乃偕之申　王素念因留駐節一日因見之嘉東　国東

君臣上下一千恭敬也來日謁箕子墓畢鄭判書偕二子諸遊

詠歸樓之西湖座間聞　國王饋迎　詔菌不勝喜躍展軸屢

矚目細閱遺而出郊五拜多士執事昔所未有百年一見今又繪

之畫是乎　國王見尊　上之義焉事大之誠焉　東國人物

數

鄉識二字大如手副使鸞清流壁三大字末端又寫盖寫二字送與遠接使等刻於浮碧樓路邊崖石上使曰須要深刻塡朱上使又寫江天勝槩四大字令刻掛於浮碧樓初上使到金郊館見遠接使所寫懸板問知是鄭判書手筆稱賛曰笔法如此而作詩何必令人替寫乎及到平壤以所題快哉亭詩有疊用字令取來改下仍令遠接使改寫旣刻訖令印出如本付頭目藏之

二十八日或晴或陰辰時兩使出坐大廳遠接使等入行禮迎慰使就前告辭兩使各給贈別詩且各付手簡使 啓于 上上使簡曰承惠迎 詔畐如獲 拱璧光彩射目 厚情遠念何以克堪一開

數　數

官亭而言乎柳枯旗亭而言乎上使答曰吾當詳錄以示遠接使又問曰詩家多使[有]閒徤字此何意乎上使曰此唐宋間方言如杜詩遮莫之類只是强徤之意又問八陣磧至今猶有舊跡乎上使曰令川峽間有如々處形制宛然又問蘇杭有葑田何此物耶兩使曰葑是水草初生可食其根聯結浮在水面元不着地其廣至如々百里土人謂之葑田是時江雨乍作或細向夕小歇長虹橫天影々射江中落日漏雲赤氣滿空天水渺々冲融一色兩使臨檻檻俯視似不忍起乘昏還館上使寫遊浮碧樓題名錄送于遠接使觀察使々刻於岩石其文曰嘉靖丁酉暮春正使龔用卿副使吳希孟同判書鄭士龍觀察使李龜齡遊此云々末端又寫

夏尚書題蒙 准請小邦不勝感戴但官本書籍歷代史記則猶在禁令我於甲午年進 表時所見書冊一切殘缺求買官本竟不能得此等禁令果出於 朝廷竊從 貴國出於他邦在廷大臣承 聖意咸欲優待安有是理安南琉球目為夷狄尚許其遣子弟入學況 貴國猶內服而不許出入耶孫郎中用心如此故宦亦不達出為知府儀制陳郎中麁我等之交友也來時陳公為設餞席謂曰 朝鮮秉禮之邦慎勿輕待此亦深許 貴國者也我等還朝說與陳公勿施禁令陳公素性謹厚必不拘孫郎中之法矣且再三語曰此事我當不忘云云遠接使又問曰古人於前輩相呼如韓文公黃九之類甚多此何意乎指

使對坐於西從容談話上使曰如今 朝廷待貴國無異內藩夏閣老
九深許之我等之來語之曰公輩雖適萬里彼既礼義之邦可以慰
羈旅之懷矣且夏閣老作詩以贈偶置遼東而來夏老參陞閣老品高代為
又曰 朝廷宰相中夏閣老文章筆法俱妙筆法則與張東海並
稱于世 國王若奏請其墨跡則 朝廷方眷夏公必喜而許之
夏老閣亦且喜矣遠接使答曰 殿下敬畏朝廷安敢仰累
聖听乎兩使曰此無妨也遠接使又謂兩使曰 本國世蒙 聖朝
寵遇朝貢使臣許自出入古今書籍任其收買近年孫郎中擅
自使提督作主事將本 國人員始令拘禁不許出入官本書籍歷
代史記毋得買賣 殿下已於先年移咨礼部乞要照舊出入

二十七日晴午後下雨在平壤上使送公文一角于甜水站辰時設餞慰宴于大廳兩使出坐遠接使觀察使及餞慰使許沆等入行礼各坐其位用女樂餞慰使先進餞慰盃遠接使等又以次行酒宴畢餞慰使就前告辞兩使令李和宗語曰　國王差送參判專為我等也今日我等留此欲尋訪古跡此事　国王必將知之矣參判與我共遊幸甚又謂遠接使觀察使曰須強留參判朝食後兩使到箕子墓焚香拜礼過井田遺墟至詠皈樓設宴方宴有　旨來到署曰天使所求迎　詔畫二件畫成送公贈云云兩使見畫驚喜即令開緘相與指點良久稱歎曰　國王用心至此不勝多謝我等當為此畫永為家寶兩使令屛卓面使稍却俱平坐於東令遠接等

尤增悚惧且私受盛礼於義未安兩使曰礼薄不稱於情毋勞謝也遠

接使仍謂上使曰所求硯面當於平安一路求覓以呈海獺皮則本非

我 國所產得之無由若果產出何至於揔買兩使發行過栽松亭

直抵大同江遠接觀察兩使等乘樓船設小酌泝流登浮碧樓行

茶礼副使謂上使曰江山之勝殆居白祥之右上使曰彼則四面俱闊此則一面

依山似不及也（以地理言之乃背山臨水上也以景槩言之乃四面俱空遠白祥上也云云）觀察使令優人設戲於庭兩使坐簷下以觀已而乘平

轎上牧丹峯峯在錦繡山之上不甚高聳而眼界甚遠四面峯巒之環

拱於遠近者畢集若培塿然時陰雲忽合微雨洒面過數刻便開霽於

帳下設小酌還下浮碧樓設宴用女樂兩使令帶來優人亦作戲於

中初昏到大同館

宴是日宴罷後兩使俱射候於廣遠樓招遠樓觀察使等令射發巡而罷上使改寫樓鳳亭額字副使寫齊安館額字付觀察使〻刻掛上使作詩贈餞慰使以別又出手簡二道付餞慰使　啓于　上使副作詩留贈餞慰使〻　達于　上又寫手簡亦令　啓達未時兩使發行至貯福院畫點夕至生陽館令退行宿所宴於明日義州人持湯站所送公文二角以來即呈于兩使

二十六日晴兩使〻家人各送紗帕一疋于遠接曰極知物薄聊以表情耳上使仍別求海獺皮硯面等物曰閣老有求之者畫硯大小各一面須令畫刻玲瓏見贈海獺皮則要以行李之物換買云〻兩使坐大廳朝飯遠接使行揖禮後告謝曰陪侍日久差失頗多常怀惶恐今反贈物

來須　詔旨悉出例外汝　國素秉礼義雖固喜賀然又能推廣
皇恩於臣民至於此極若非　殿下之賢不能及此我等回去當奏
達于　朝廷云云又曰地志模得甚備深謝皇意當久玩不置且諸相
佳作亦多謝云云兩使又謂遠接使曰自今日為始須勿用女樂遠接使
等答曰　殿下差遣餞慰使設宴於此此事皆出於
殿下之意今若不用則餞慰使將何辭以復命於
在樂今日聽我等之言不用女樂是乃敬也餞慰使立於兩使前
懇請陳樂兩使良久商議乃曰即今為判書等官要設我等帶
來之樂一再奏枝之後當聽女樂之用遂令頭目兩人執樂而奏
一人着假面為戲其類凡五人仍與　本國女樂迭奏可前以終其

送于境務要慰我等之心何必爲齋日而捐今日之歡乎多上使語遠
接使曰欲見東方建國世系歷年等事幸煩書示
二十五日陰令譯官呈遠接觀察兩使及平山府使等榜目于兩使又呈
畧書東方建国歷年小錄上使又手寫小紙送于遠接使曰鄉試每科各
道所取多少用何人作考官何處差來用幾貟考官以希備示遠接使
即令寫送曰文科試鄉八道揔取二百人臨開試觀察使具由啓 聞差
委在京文官考試每一道四貟辰時餞慰宴于廣遠樓兩使出坐
遠接觀察兩使及餞慰使金光轍等入行禮畢呈昨日京來地志及
開城餞慰使等和答詩篇仍以有 旨內百官加階別舉取人錫宴
臣僚等事告于兩使兩使相顧驚喜答曰 皇帝之生天下同慶

少歇晝點到棘城行茶礼登道上高丘望海指九月山問曰此山何名譯
官以實對申時到黃州簇錦溪乘樓船見所題詩篇及額字頗有
喜色就設小酌謂平山府使李霖曰汝爲何年出身對曰甲申年出身
也上使曰子午卯酉既爲式年則又何云甲申年耶答曰　本國於試年
之外特設别科取人謂之别試上使問之年李霖曰弘治辛酉之歲霖以
生上使曰可謂少年登科也欲見榜目到州館書以示我兩使見遠接使
及觀察使卓上不設魚肉問其故遠接等答曰今日乃
先王后齋日也夕至客館令還行餞慰宴于明朝兩使登廣遠樓相與投
壺爲戱副使又射候數巡招遠接觀察兩使共射遠接使等辭曰
今日乃　先王后齋日也請於明朝乃射上使曰　殿下令諸君伴

今

目中本不開載兩使曰然則從其制録亦兩使又曰前後女樂之設已知國王慰客之誠矣明日黃州之宴請勿用也遠接使答曰餞慰使奉殿下之命來慰大人不可自擅然當共議之副使送詩數篇其中憶秦娥一篇乃歌詞也遠接使以音律不同不次其韻副使索和頗急遠接使答曰　本國與　中國語音殊異歌曲之類尤不相似今雖强和必不成腔往年祈郎中到此之時製歌詞十餘篇伴接徐宰相(居正)一切和答只是押韻而已未免音節之異故今不敢和也

二十四日陰辰時兩使出坐大廳遠接觀察兩使入行揖禮(兩使曰)欲見兩宰相榜目須速取示副使又出所寫樂山亭額字以給兩使步往棲鳳亭覽觀景物仍歷入遠接使下處循階看紅芍藥而去即發行至洲里院

令

接使令洪謙告曰未時忙遽付諸都監以未不意鋟刻時失真至於不
勝惶恐々々令雖補畫恐亦非真若蒙更寫則當令觀察使付之巧匠上使
曰俟到前頭當寫送兩使自發程以後凡到館驛觀其所題懸板雖一
邊一畫有差輒令改補且舉其道上吟詠不係館驛之詩謂遠接使
曰此詩何獨不刻乎須趁夜刻板明朝示我云々遠接使不得已歷寫所
作送于前路令預刻以待夕行宿所宴于大廳兩使語遠接使曰前
前日 國王所送會試小錄雖佳有未詳盡我等欲知榜目規制不
須多錄只錄一二榜來亦可矣如某年試某人居甲通一榜幾人原籍
親名年歲一々備錄而來我等到此備見文物之盛獨不知科目之制
豈不有虧違 啓國王詳錄示我遠接使答曰年歲則本 国於榜

十矣皆不能中亦令遠接使及觀察使射之移時乃罷上使先令設幕
於所名翠屏山下未時兩使至幕次招遠接使及觀察使相與臨岸
而坐令車允成傳語于觀察使曰若構亭於此真可以添漢山物色又
戲曰我輩當為此山於封太守之後更作歆羨而來副使執盃喝左
右曰此雲岡學士翠屏山酒也勉勿留殘遂發行至安城館晝點
乘夕至龍泉館令退行宿所宴于明朝
二十三日晴晨時兩使坐龍泉館前山岸帳幕就設宴卓副使射候亦
令遠接使觀察使以射之仍行酒礼而罷兩使發行至劒水館點晝
後到鳳山兩使步至樓鳳亭觀扁額上使曰字体多失本真且職銜
斜殊不可觀遂令承吏用黑補其字畫送于遠接使可依此補之遠

投壺爲戲仍令遠接使及觀察使共校且設小酌而罷夕至寶山館
設宿所宴于大廳兩使出坐遠接使與觀察使入行揖禮仍呈會試小
錄兩使看罷曰甚好〻〻且謂遠接使曰我等前日出京之稿初非手錄也
寫字人等多致誤書有落字處今欲考校以還須無遺送來又曰遂
日設宴賓主俱勞今日之宴願乞停行遂揖辭而入夜上使將其詩稿
校勘數帖先送于遠接使

二十二日晴辰時兩使發行至葱秀山先往碑石處觀覽遂如川上由假橋
渡川坐崖下排細賞翫招遠接使及觀察使設酌兩使相與射覆爲
戲上使約曰我輸則我與判書飮罰吳老輸則吳與觀察使飮罰
兩使互相勝負各飮五六盃而止已而命設小酌兩使共射副使稍發五六

乘夕至興義館退行宿所宴于明朝

二十三日晴辰時設宴于大廳兩使出坐遠接使與觀察使入行禮告以二十日未到有 旨而載聞筆資之意且呈物件單字兩使答曰於慶會樓及 勤政殿 國王所贈禮物皆不敢受至於細碎之物不之却者不欲違國王之誠懇也然亦心常未安今又追送此物於路上尤所不安於心豈可受乎遠接使再三懇說兩使曰 國王誠意至此若固拒則恐以我等有所不平也各受白苧布黑麻布各五疋曰要以領誠而已遂布字賚來通事李永貞還饋飯羹遠接使令李和宗等將京來人情物件給與高嵩等且說禮曹開字之意嵩高等答曰今次賚去甚難乞於謝恩使入來時付送云云巳時兩使發行猶離坐樓船柏遠接使及觀察使

梓

字送與遠接使曰可付坡州官使之刻掛云辰時兩使發行至狻猊驛
坐驛東二里許路邊帳幕處開城人領捕魚作欄以放之兩使臨觀
觀賞既而悉放之於川午到金郊館晝點即發行至吾助川兩使沿
川上下良久觀景就坐川邊幕次招遠接使及觀察使共坐仍設小酌
上使問此處有笛吹者乎答曰無矣仍令頭目等以登川上岩崖弄吹
笛或吹嘴甫食頃而罷上使謂觀察使曰我之翠屛山記曾作懸板否
答曰已鋟梓掛之矣上使曰木板易朽要須壽諸石然後乃可久矣
觀察使與遠接使同議答曰此意甚可但非我等自擅之事當
啓於 殿下上使曰若立碑石宜印數十本分寄吾兩人方見諸 君之信
矣且華皇集印出通印前人稿集且須不拘舊例優数以送云云

殿下勿用之教況内臣奉　殿下之命来餞于此不敢自擅兩使曰然則
姑聽諸君之請黄琢(音行)先餞慰杯餞慰(使)次進畢又與遠接使等各行
酒禮而罷頭目高嵩高康鎮等自前越江以後持單字言曰此遼東
大人之求請也遠接使不信其言不曾　啓達自回程以来逐日来
說願聞回報之辭去

二十日晴

高崇(嵩)等所傳遼東大人求請單字及　天使到義州欲觀統軍亭(則)領次
處之兩使坐大廳謂餞慰使等曰前日　殿下許(諾)遼地志及登科錄今(具書狀上送)
何不来耶歸告　殿下以俺等佇待之意兩使各作詩贈兩餞慰使
上使又出慶會樓歌一篇付餞慰使使献于　上副使寫滴翠亭額

基

遠接使曰月李石暮春欲觀故跡夫後人勿許放散遠接使答曰城中古跡
皆已荒殘無足可觀且街路湫隘前後 詔使無有游覽者上使怒
曰但當導我去路而已何相告禁遂屏騎從乘平轎而出遠接使與
觀察使留守同議先令由人徑路設帳幕於滿月臺須臾兩使至宰
譯官及頭目等步登後並周覽殆遍良久乃下遠接使請設小酌回
推而起上使謂李和宗曰宮墓甚大而何無城址乎和宗答曰爲因
歲久頹圮無存耳遂促還館晡時設餞慰宴兩使出坐餞慰使
許洽別餞慰使黃琦與遠接使及觀察使留守等入行禮後
以次坐於西壁既開宴將陳女樂上使曰昨日已告不用女樂之意判
書亦云依命而今日復用何如遠接使答曰昨雖聞命時無

距

館以後傺令退行宿所宴于明朝上使令譯官傳於語遠接使曰此處無翱鍠乎何不供進頓轉行前路使預辦

十九日陰

朝令譯官呈沈判書所製詩于兩使看過曰得見好詩多謝辰時設宴于大廳上使曰我等初來之時享用女樂正以貴國爲 詔書致優禮且重違 國王厚意故也今已事完多領 貴國之誠今後始自開城府以下勿復用女樂兩使發行至招賢院坐幕次即曰此處既無堂宇何必久坐遂上轎從行遠接使告曰開城距此尚十六七里廚人告已備乞於轎前進茶盤兩使曰判書慰賓客之意至此誠不忍辭速取來即於轎上啜茶畢而行未時兩使到開城府即使李和宗謹

數

王之候臣曰如〻至焉王之情文之典曰數至焉迨甚過也謙虛沖雅知不
勝細皆酒以灌候度尊朝廷也桑扈曰左之右之無不宜之右之左之無
不宜之全言才也酒酣曰愷悌君子民之父母言能民也南山曰樂只君子
邦家之光言盡臣節而增重之也夫以有左右之才而盡民之責則
其爲邦家之光必矣碧蹄金相之餞也東望實懸〻焉禮無老
謝垂亮華甚副使臨發指絲花團曰有我老親欲以此一朶歸示已時冬
行至坡州書壁兩使上東軒前小亭觀覽上使謂譯官曰吳老參欲
名此亭滴翠云申時發行至臨津日欲沒矣兩使上江邊亭子觀所
寫亭額須臾乃就船呼遠棲使及觀察使共坐仍設酌漁人網得鯉
魚數尾兩使令取繩繫鼻沉之於江相與臨江喜笑乘夜至東坡

又以次各行酒禮訖兩使就房少歇居無何上使又出來與左議政
等叙立而語謂曰貴國君送謝　恩使須延一箇月待我等回　京
之日使之發程可也左議政作贈別詩呈于兩使兩使稱謝曰真大
手也上使又曰貴國海味雖多未解調飪之方是大欠也吾當開錄
以送上使亦慕華館餞別詩且修簡一道付左議政使　啓于
上其簡曰天涯之會夢想不及累承　賢藩款接深見　雅情昭石
蹄館諸官之来尤荷厚宴顧鄙人何以堪之惟增銘刻耳別後
更希　道体養和錫國遐福以慰遠望小錄志書冀　叅惠
及實大願也顒候　賢王世子均此致懷副亦附簡以送曰不穀
辱有　明命朝鮮之役雅忝是惧太平之館也　王屢至焉

謂不屬此館故使不之刻也且原稿其時 啓子 殿下令雜
欲刻不能誦憶上使即送稿曰吾詩固拙若不刻掛則後來 詔使
何從知今日之事乎須速入梓示我於前路然後送掛於此上使又取
前日途中所作雜詩用筆點註令各於附近驛館亭院一切懸掛
遠接使即寫碧蹄館詩使刻之又寫沿途所作刻板時西遺
漏者移文於前路各官使之趁期刻掛
十八日晴遠接使與左議政禮曹判書俱和兩使在太平館及發漢城
所作之詩寫單啓呈上使曰都是佳作多謝〻〻 辰時設餞慰宴于
大廳兩使出坐左議政坐東遠接使及禮曹判書觀察使都承旨
俱坐西都承旨先行餞慰盃左議政礼曹判書次之右議政以下

朴守良請留兩使曰春天本來多雨安可避也權杜已去尤不可留

已而 上又遣禮曹叅判金光轍請留未及傳語聞又遣右議

政尹殷輔請留兩使答曰 殿下厚意固已知悉但行止已定不

可中止也時發行慕華館 上已設宴待之兩使入館受餞宴良

久乃出 上出送大門又設小酌訖即發行至洪濟院招遠接使及

館伴共坐仍於坐中作詩以贈館伴酒礼既畢乃出乘夜至碧石

歸館 上親遣左議政金安老[illegible]礼曹判書尹仁鏡餞慰於此

別遣都承旨朴洪鱗亦來餞慰兩使夜深退行餞禮於明日

上使令譯官語遠接使我留於此館因 國王候問之意作謝

詩一律令何不掛他作而廿此一篇耶遠接使答曰果有其詩但[illegible]

馬步追故是日先驅頭目等追慕次皆下馬趨去未時兩使入城至
景福宮　上率百官如儀行禮訖　上改服陞殿行茶禮而罷兩使遂
至太平館安歇　上即幸太平館行下馬宴夜半乃罷
十一日晴在太平館
十二日晴在太平館
十三日晴在太平館
十四日晴在太平館
十五日晴在太平館
十六日晴在太平館
十七日雨兩使臨發而勢不止　上先幸慕華館遣同副承旨

主而 殿下為賓當讓 殿下使坐於北我等却坐於南至若設
宴之時則我國賓也當從北坐賓坐 殿下國主也當從南坐主
坐若是則賓主各得其禮矣其旨如此禮曹佐郎朴自英來稟
曰謄黄 聖旨分付一二人直送大平館則是如尋常衙門文書無
異矣今欲別差官人畧具儀仗護至大平館兩使曰既非勅書安可
用如此之禮遂令頭目等領至大平館遠接使李(荇)一人負先至慕華
館肅拜仍 啓達洪謙而誦兩絶句 上引見閤一路旁謝兩使書
點後發行踰沙峴置 詔書於迎詔門下而分立其左右
上於慕華館門前官道上幕次行五拜三叩頭禮遂乘輦先尋
還宮兩使曾在洪濟院戒頭目等曰 殿下在幕次時汝等若帶

而發矣遠接使即修書狀送于政院右承旨金瑬來問安且言曰今日
上幸慕華館終日待候之意夕行留日遠接使與觀察使如例進酒而罷
初十日晴平明兩使坐大廳共飯已已即發行至德水川邊帳幕處暫歇
茶果巳時至洪濟院禮曹判書尹仁鏡及都監郎廳等已來候于此
上使與副使同議于寫單字呼遠接使謂之曰前日儀註草已有送
令而思之其中有非禮之事故今寫與單使之曉釋因令遠接使讀
之讀罷曰可急報 殿下與通行之正禮若不依此則吾等不可赴宴
矣云云其大要謂賓主之位當分南北而坐今東西而坐實非正禮須
詔之後於殿中茶禮時則制俾繞取賓北主南而未安權依儀註
賓於東而主於西可也至於太平館相會之時則館我之安下處我為

其狀兩使具冠帶出坐大廳遠接使進前行揖禮仍面言曰恩詔齎
到國門 殿下率臣民祗候所當急迎 聖詔但雨勢轉大必不開
霽在 殿下豈憚出候誠恐大禮有觸事體上使曰我等萬里擎
詔今到國門而留心不自安故初意欲趁雨霽便即入 京今與副使商
量雨既不霽畢於須慶之時未免倉皇已決意留宿急報
國王遠接使曰明日雨猶不止則何以處之上使曰到得其時當更議之遠
接使即修書狀送于政院右承旨黃憲來問安仍請於十日入 京
未及告禀間 宣傳官朴鐵壽來謂黃憲曰當告天使曰旅館草〻
强留使華實爲未安今日行止須任兩大人之意黃憲即以此言告
兩使答曰今日則業已停行日亦已晩不可更計明日則雨雖不止當冒雨

雖何事猶奈爾之語鶯流鴨笑教人共一回山色濛濛畫已昏望叢林

深處鵲拜喧海潮似是春山雨小浦平添過水痕是夜兩政丞及

禮曹判書兩承旨皆還去

初九日猶雨在碧蹄館平明上使起寢李和宗因家人徵稟行止上使

大怒叱其家人曰行止在我何煩相問我欲徐觀雨勢以定之何擅稟

外言食頃出坐廳外李和宗進曰昨昏有更說鄭判書使之飛報

之命故敢稟行止上使曰此去 王京四十里雨勢若歇則我豈能坐

此且到洪濟院改服之時後 殿下尚可及來李和宗反覆言遑遽

未便之意上使怒而不答遠接使即修書狀送于該院辰時上使以便

服就副使房談話遠接使欲親問行止就其外面伺候令 譯官告

前者以迎 詔重事故擇吉日得初九日十一日等日明日既不得迎 詔故敢以十一日爲稟耳上使與副使低頭商議良久乃答曰奉 詔書留住於此心實未安明日當前到洪濟院或慕華館等處宿歇待雨晴行禮則於 國王雖未亦得其便矣李和宗卽答曰洪濟慕華二字俱無屋舍只是空廳不可安下兩使曰然則明朝雨若不霽我等當依汝言留住於此若向晴則當卽入京歸告 殿下以雨之霽不霽料我之行不行也明朝我亦更說鄭劉書使之飛報上使一頭目在東軒傳寫上使所製詩篇通事洪謹從其後窺見誦得兩絶句其一曰溪水灣灣柳色新驅車鎭日逐紅塵

日明日洪濟院見大臣之來且到 王府親見 殿下誠懇方爾定奪右議政既退遠接使觀察使行揖禮而出上使就副使房共假說行迎慰宴安李和宗告兩使曰預宴官既多西壁窄了不可盡坐敢稟兩使曰令國相特坐於東舊例 天使到碧蹄政丞來慰座在西壁許坐於東從今始也都承旨先進迎慰杯領議政禮曹判書以次進盃說領議政以下復以次行酒宴未畢右副承旨黃璿來蓋請留 天使於此待來十日入京事也宴罷即告曰 國王遣承旨兩使曰可速呼來黃璿進前行禮令李和宗告曰兩勢如此明日迎詔恐未成禮 殿下別遣內臣請兩大人强留兩日來十日入京

殆無以加國人頌之天下稱之以為美談於此可見我 皇上車書一統
之盛化行於遠我等將敬聞於 上以彰其賢也併附書此
初八日陰午後下雨辰時兩使發行至臨津招遠攝使及觀察使共坐
舡上設小酌酒數巡漁人獻鯉魚若干尾兩使臨舷而立用繩繫
魚背沉之於水以觀其游泳未時到坡州晝點日昃乃發冒雨至
碧蹄館領議政金謹思 禮曹判書尹仁鏡以迎慰使已到此都承旨朴洪鱗
以別迎慰事右議政尹殷輔以留 詔 王宮事亦來行迎 詔禮後
兩使各就房已而出坐大廳領議政先入拜謁而出右議政尹殷輔以留
詔 王宮事亦來行迎 詔禮後兩使各就房已而出坐大廳領議
政告入拜謁而出右議政次入仍令李和宗告留 詔王宮事啓

立　葵

中查勘其事併究責鎮巡三司等官有何事情從實回報此與汝
國之事無預是以不録來看今禮部見有題稿在其 賜禮物一節前
日已備言之我等將行特聞 朝廷御文華殿召閣老禮部親說此事
聖意謂此 詔只是報 皇子生與天下一例比之冊封諸事不同所以禮
部本中請禮物只批答另行所謂另行者有所待之辭也 聖意
蓋謂待後冊主〻 皇太子之時别有所 賜矣大要如此今日開來儀
註適閱之喟然歎曰此非所謂秉禮義之國乎曾聞齊桓公蔡〻丘之
會周天子致侯伯之胙王人致命令桓公無下拜桓公答曰天威不違顔
咫尺余小白敢貪天子之威 命方令 天子明 聖皇靈廣布大非周
天子之時之比而汝 國王素稱秉禮實過於桓公暴華尊 上之誠

簇子若干軸務要長廣可急造作我等雖留三日其間可及造矣又曰
前請平壤留亦須毋忘初昏行宿所宴兩使曰堂中狹窄不用進膳
只速遞酒宴罷遠接使即以 下諭吉時告于兩使答曰當於平明發
行遠接使又請曰若於平明發行則恐不及吉時須 詔兩使曰然
則當於五更頭發行上使出一單字付遠接使曰安南國須 詔等來
恐譯者未能盡傳故錄此以示其文曰述口說以代譯者之傳庶易曉也
初差官往汝國來皆出 朝廷聖意此原無舊例前所謂以一統之
禮待汝 國王正謂此也本與安南國同欲遣官後禮部查覆稱安
南國中自相構亂數年朝貢不通當另差人往問以此只差汝 國中
來也因此不差翰林與科往安南國別差錦衣衛指揮一員往彼國

予上使曰 詔書之意我等亦豈能詳知到內閣暫見 詔草大槩興誠
布四方之意同其中有若干殊異之節遠接使又問曰禮部題本內有往
諭 朝鮮安南知悉之語未審亦遣 詔使於安南乎 兩使曰禮部元本
雖云其後以安南國中自相構亂罷本停之且 頒賜之事則閣老等議
以今者只諭 大慶之意不必有 賜待冊封頒 詔時該有賞賜云之
問禮官任翀亨改儀註來到呈于兩使旦告曰郊外行五拜三叩頭之禮
本非洪武年頒降儀註之禮故削此 天使之來並無此儀今者兩大
人以謂 天下通行之禮欲令施行 殿下特從大人之言改儀註以送
兩使曰多謝 賢王秉禮而時 兩使到東坡館上使令李和宗傳語
曰我等於一路所賞山川樓亭皆有紀述矣到 王京即當寫示堂

用鄉等題稱齎捧 詔書前往 朝鮮國諭知恐彼 國王請留
詔書乞要比照正德年間修撰倫文叙等事例聽其請留一節既查
有前例相應議處合候 命下本部行令各官臨時斟酌如彼
國王請留之意果出誠懇亦宜俯順其情聽其請留緣係 大慶及奉
欽依禮部着了來說事理未敢擅便謹題請旨奉 聖旨是兩使又
令李和宗傳 語曰儒生迎 詔事前日問禮官已報講定此府大慶也
兩儒生何不迎 詔乎遠接使答曰儒生迎 詔非在前恒為之事今因
大人之命特令迎 詔但時未見儀註而來故此處儒生未及迎 詔國
學儒生則自當迎 詔矣午時到招賢院 兩使招遠接使及觀察使同飲
遠接使問曰前承 皇帝親製 詔書之語果與頒海內 詔旨有異

中吳希孟俱有點其一道曰翰林院等衙門修撰等官龔用卿等
題爲 大慶事內開欽蒙差充正副使齎捧 詔書往諭朝鮮
國王仰見我 皇上推六合一家之心廣九州無外之化甚盛也正起行
間思得所捧 詔書到彼國中萬一國王姓諱尊上之心出於誠懇
請留 詔書以爲鎮國之寶雖其慕華向化之誠固稱秉禮然未
奉有 明旨不敢擅專若待彼時奏 聞則道里往還動經旬朔不
無有誤爲此合先題 請如蒙乞 勅下該部比照正德年間修撰
倫文叙編脩沈燾等差往安南事例聽其請留庶 朝廷大典有
所遵守而外國人心有所取信矣具本題奏 聖旨禮部看了來說
其一道曰禮部一本 大慶事內開看得翰林院等衙門修撰等官龔

字內載三道公文其一道曰禮部尚書夏言一本 大慶事嘉靖十五年
十月初六日恭遇 皇嗣誕生例該 詔誥天下本部已經題本 欽依
着十一月初六日彌月之期舉行欽此遵外伏蒙 皇上面諭 皇子
初生既 詔告天下何獨外國至冊封日始遣使 詔諭況已告聞天
下百神使當使一体知悉他日冊立一并行 詔告鄉宜議擬舉行所
據本月初六日 頒降告 皇太子生 詔書合無依冊立 皇太子
例遣翰林院官一員充正使給事中一員充副使齎捧 詔書往諭
朝鮮安南二國知悉候 冊皇太子之日一并行遣使 詔諭合候
命下本部欽遵舉行奉 聖旨是着為令禮部一本大慶事奉
聖旨着有點的去 賜國王綵段另行 翰林院修撰龔用卿户科給事

詳

朴守良等俱坐西壁京来妓生樂工等奏樂於前兩使曰我等因忙常感發兩
禮況用女樂乎朴守良進前使譯官告曰　殿下別遣內臣帶来于此要助宴
席令若却之則實孤　殿下之意也兩使曰業已来矣姑令奏樂令後用女
樂之時先稟我等可也朴守良先進迎慰盃柳世麟次進說兩使曰日晩
行忙諸君不用常禮各進一盃宴畢朴守良進曰留　詔事兩大人既題准兩
來乞於須　詔之後即留　王宮答曰此事須見　國王誠懇乃可聽也
到㫌歸更見大臣商量告之兩使各就房已而會立大廳招遠接使及
兩迎慰使觀察使留守於前授一單字曰此我等謄黄　聖旨之首尾
也非欲以此單呈於　國王也欲令諸君詳〻看轉　啓耳語已兩迎慰
使辭退兩使曰委送兩宰臣来慰於此　賢王誠意多謝〻〻其單

慶尚道東萊縣山川甚秀麗得無模寫彼處耶答曰是矣兩使指點良
久曰真好景也遠接使令李和宗告兩使曰今夕當宿于開城府初十日東坡
初八日碧蹄館初九日入　王京前路宿所如此敢稟行止兩使曰我等已知
消日當依所言而行晝點後發行至狻猊驛開城府設帳幕於路傍高
丘兩使下轎暫歇進茶啖既罷至迎賓館京畿觀察使金希銳都事
李塘開城留守韓允昌經歷安宇都事金橫及執事守令等迎
詣于館前申時入府迎慰使柳世麟別迎慰使朴守良及府官守令等官
分東西班行迎　詣禮後遠接使又與迎慰使等官行私禮而出兩使曰
今日日暮身倦迎慰宴退行明朝可也夕副使取溫湯沐浴于房
初七日晴辰時設迎慰宴於大廳兩使出坐遠接使與柳世麟韓允昌金希銳

其祖嘗爲司諫院獻納有諫諍之功故錄其子孫也上使曰真箇好法度也遠接使令譯官告兩使以造送涼轎之意兩使皆喜初昏副使招金山海語曰慈秀山越峯龔老爹嗟賞不已名曰翠屛亦有著述汝但心記姑勿語判書

初六日晴兩使坐大廳受宿所宴巳時乘涼轎發行到吾助川下轎周覽曰向來所經山川無如此絶好回來當穩賞而去又謂李和宗曰今乘涼轎甚佳和宗曰殿下慮氈轎日暖故特令該官造送耳兩使相視曰 國王計料之賢至於此也呼押來官來吾欲面謝以送和宗曰押來官昨夕將轎子交割卽還矣午時到金郊館兩使立於大廳見屛間有黃鶴樓姑蘇臺二畫問曰此畫貴國何處乎通事洪謙對曰 本國慶尚道有此樓臺上使曰聞判書貫在

所持棍杖誤觸張仝之頭全聲曰彼守門者打我遂告於上使遠接使聞之
令平山府使李霖拿究守門者頗用嚴刑仍械杻囚置於庭辰時上使出
坐大廳受宿所宴畢命招守門者謂之曰汝信打張全則罪不細矣今聞汝
兩人俱相戲謔是本無有意於打遂令放送巳時兩使發行到平山府前小
院下轎坐院食頃即出至金巖館晝點上使〻李和宗問遠接使曰聽見
葱秀山少東峯巒奇峭遠勝葱秀甚名謂何遠接使答曰我國多山如彼
比者無數豈有名乎俗或通謂之葱秀山申時兩使到猪灘下轎坐灘邊帳
幕進酒數巡觀察使呈各種海物兩使稱謝即上樓舡以渡乘夕到瑞興義
館令退行宿所宴于明日上使方飯見進止差使員等指長連縣監成
栝文此官為何等出身金山海答曰從門蔭以進上使曰門蔭云何答曰

流泉發興忘返觀察使進海族諸種其中有〻甲大小石花上使見之甚喜
取小石花一盤令頭目具甲燒之於前招遠接使及觀察使令地坐而自踞
踏掌取石花用小刀擘開食之每食揖好隨擘隨食積甲滿盤仍分與遠
接使觀察使等戲語曰宰相輩居蜊蝗產出之地而不解燒食可笑巡酒四
五盃而止且曰家在海濱實慣食此吾鄉距　帝都八千里今又東來其積萬
餘里與諸君得諧賞於此豈非有數副使曰福建實大海之堧琉球占城皆
密邇往來吾鄉乃常州也在楊子江邊與福建相去一月餘程云州官等令
鷹人放鷹逐雉雉披而墮又捕生麞以進兩使皆拍手失喜日沒時到寶山
館未及館下轎改服以入令退宿所宴于明朝
初五日晴上使頭目張全年十七戲索帶子於本館守門者因與相持守門者

初四日晴巳時兩使坐太廳受宿所宴語遠接使曰吾觀皇華集龍泉館南
江最為勝地董侍講到觀捉雉興作詩紀之我等今日當過慈秀山行
忙不可久住當暫過飲茶而行遠接使答曰本道觀察使已修治設供帳矣
宴罷兩使即就南江循除觀水良久就坐命進茶果飲茶一巡又令斟
酒曰本欲飲茶而已吳老爹請飲三盃故耳且從容語遠接使曰先輩往
遊之地吾輩來踐旧跡得非幸乎即發行午到安城館晝點促行到慈秀
山兩使步上董侍講石記前讀過數遍嗟歎不已謂李和宗曰 國
王何不於此建碑閣乎此特小費耳且碑面多殘缺何也和宗答曰無知
打柴之人擊打致缺我 殿下令拿究治罪姑護以藩籬耳看訖即
步下水次幞裹着褻服穿鞋步匝水次無數又由路杓渡水看叢濱

盡獨此禮不行是所謂舍其大而圖其細者也況 詔書初至汝

國王見君之始尤當盡禮使國人傳說汝國王盡敬 朝廷之

意然後汝 國人知盡敬汝 國之禮乃此義事也非導汝以失禮也今天子

待汝 國王與天下一體汝 國中行禮乃與天下異同是自外也我等聞

汝 國王素賢且守禮義之國入境以來每事盡善故不惜此一言

汝歸語 國王但求其心之安則禮得矣我等所言非分別之爭理外

之求也但以汝國禮失此不行爲可惜爾今日聞汝 國令各處生

負迎 詔甚喜、此非守禮義國之不能行耳 朝廷聞之亦必深嘉

眷注之心日益加矣晡時兩使上門樓眺望乘昏至龍泉館令退宿一所

宴于明日

詔之禮付問禮官其文曰連日與禮官講禮恐譯者傳言未真故
特以此示之今天下親王併各官迎　詔郊外俱先行五拜三叩頭禮
畢然後前導至　國中及各衙門自有開讀儀汝禮官前日所開
儀註俱是但此一節今日所論非改儀註也正謂儀註開載未盡
耳況此禮天下通行之汝　國中獨不行是有二禮也同一　天子
之　詔同一天子之臣而豈可有二禮乎且如我於前日未時經過各
處參贊判書及觀察使等官皆鞠躬道左我等不之責者此猶
有說以　詔書尚未開讀也今既至汝國中矣　國王猶行此
鞠躬之禮可乎若如汝所言則汝　國王亦不用前導可也今既前
導矣又三舞蹈矣又十二拜矣何獨靳此郊之禮而不行乎餘禮既

傳布也遠接使又問今次路上行酒之禮與儀註各異之意則兩
使曰路上享禮行酒則出於一時權宜汝　國中享儀則當依　本
國舊規唐學士時行禮儀註可一依爲之問禮官謁兩使告曰五
拜三叩頭之禮不載洪武年頒降儀註其後　朝廷不須別撰儀
註我　國世守舊禮不可遽改　兩使曰此禮乃天下通行之正禮不
可廢也汝　國常稱慕習華制不學如此正禮而習何等禮乎須
詔之儀不但在於洪武年間如永樂宣德年間皆經頒降汝　國
歷考旧典而無所闕漏耶例獨謬執洪武年旧制乎今次　詔書
國王若開見則必待　朝廷優待之意誠敬之心自然而生然往復
講論只憑譯舌誠有所未盡者當分釋寫給　上使遂寫郊外迎

連用大盃勸觀察使用中盃勸遠接使曰今日欲知酒户多少且饋射
官酒又招一行通事醫員等各饋酒日晚發行至劒水館晝點問禮
官任弼亨前夕已到宿于此遠接使擧京來有 旨之意問于兩使
答曰 勑書皆我等奏准謄黃只管我等奉行不干汝 國臨須
詔時當令我等帶來人賫擎直送于下處不煩汝 國護衛且曰
令次 詔書異於常格 皇帝親自御製文 詔旨欄界皆用金龍
李閣老特謂我等曰我從前未嘗見如此寵異之 詔今開讀
則 國王必知朝廷深愛之意亦當踊躍矣凡 詔書須訖還
納例也從 國王願留與否處之事奉 聖旨而來若留 詔而
去則真是鎮國之寶至於 詔書事意則於開讀之前固不當

取供酉時至鳳山 上使曰今日氣困宿所宴退行明朝可也上使步至松間草亭又邀副使散步松陰轉往梨花樹下取投壺相對以戲仍酌酒相勸二更乃罷 上使招李和宗問曰此行來官無乃有唐史時參差任者乎和宗知 天使見皇華集以問答曰今遠接使鄭判書及平壤迎慰使蘇判書皆其時都監官也上使曰孰爲內資寺正乎蓋其時遠接使爲內資寺正故云也

初三日晴辰時行宿所宴畢兩使各就房遠接使與觀察使同議令李和宗請兩使曰今日乃三月三日也 國俗例作艾餅登山遊宴客館南頂構一草亭最高豁可以望遠頗暫駐 行旌兩使曰諾遂至頂與遠接使及觀察使共坐草亭設小酌令射官等射侯 上使

取雜種魚皆問鄉名質以華語又令燒蒸於前以進 上使見進魚時不進於遠接使及觀察使問其故遠接使令譯士對曰今日乃先王忌日上下共守齋素耳兩使曰汝 國制禮動似朝廷朝廷享萬歲則汝國亦享萬歲矣上使囑副使名川及樓船副使名川曰簇錦溪名樓船曰搖雲上使謂遠接使曰 貴國文物規爲及尊俎禮讓一如中朝海外之邦誰得與比偉者吾兩人每歎賑不已且曰前路有傑山秀水可以供眼底者皆欲翫賞而去判書豈不知我等意乎未時就途到蘇城院小歇即行未數里下轎登山頂望海到沙里院晝點上使令李和宗傳語曰此地近海如蜊蝗蚌蛤等鮮味宜連日責來副使曰龔老爹家在海濱慣食海味各種新鮮告判書續

宴于明日

三月初一日晴辰時兩使出坐大廳受宿所宴〻已發行至貯福院接遠接

使會坐大廳共畫點茶啖未時到黃州黃〻海道觀察使李億孫及州

官差使員等迎〻詣于五里程優人轉車上彩棚來迎行至大門外

兩使駐轎觀彩棚雜戲入大廳立迎慰使金麟孫與觀察使都事守

令等分東西班行迎　詣禮〻已又行私禮而罷平壤人持投壺以來

兩使俱坐東軒投箭數巡夕設迎慰宴迎慰使與遠接使及觀察使

各行酒禮迎慰使欲更行酒兩使曰我等俱倦不必更飮當於

王京漢江會面矣

初二日晴兩使發行到於草川坐樓船接遠接使同載仍設小酌且命捕魚

使又請樓船名上使曰宜名以濟川通事洪謙曰 王京有濟川亭
上使囑副使改之副使曰名以乘鷁可也行當寫額以給未時下船坐
岸上小幕又令漁人撒網取魚移時乃發過大井兩使下轎俯視久々
至中和生陽館即令移東軒賓華於大門前招射官等射弓一巡又
令頭目取炬一把立於四十步之外用紅紙作鵠貼於炬腹令射之龍
川郡守曹世鳳義州軍官徐慶千各中一矢又招頭目試弩射官
等弓子酉時乃罷上使謂李和宗曰此館有投壺乎答曰平壤府有
之上使曰須速取來上使曰有屋轎褁以氈帳春日漸暖可作單帳那
遠接使即令中和郡守造鴉青木綿單帳以京來八帶魚呈于上
使上使曰形樣甚奇吾地方只有八稍魚未有此耳兩使令退行宿所

留則聽欽此遂謄黃 聖旨以來其一 勅則奉使萬里安可無
防身之道以此亦奉 聖旨而來又問曰 勅書既不干 本國則當
無迎 勅之儀〻註內亦當不錄乎答曰迎 勅之事今次果無矣儀
註內則雖并錄有何妨焉禮所不當爲則固不可錄也禮所當爲
則何必拘於一時之無而闕其典乎副使招譯官傳語于遠接使曰昨
日所失扇子門子誤摺在蟒衣間今乃尋出矣因擧以示之已時兩
使發行到大東同江樓船稱賞形勝因指船上板墻箕城畵曰此處
必有畵手將昨日迎 詔及我等來此遊賞之狀車馬塡咽候送之
形到 王京令工畵者繪作一通各贈我等以爲後日玩賞幸甚拜〻
語之兩使又曰練光亭風月樓額字時無楷法回來時當寫給觀察

接使令差使員等搜索竟不能得移文觀察使之搜覓副使在房内手
寫一紙付金山海送於遠接使曰假如義州一州之内有某館有某山有某
水有某溪巖江疑寺宇之名有某事實遺蹟之類凡至　王京歷所州
郡當爲我一一開陳之假如義州有義順館良策館所串館下面亦當
音註因何而得名山水之類皆然

三十日晴辰時兩使出坐大廳設迎慰宴遠接使與迎慰使各行酒禮用女樂
宴後稟曰來月初九日乃迎　詔吉日也敢稟答曰此事正好雨則行一站晴
則倍程要及此日入京又問勅書二道所以不干本國之意答曰已盡言之
何更問也凡　詔書既頒之後還納御府例也我等以賫擎　詔書當
依例賫還或留與本　國等因具題禮部奉　聖旨本國若欲

李龜齡及府官差使員等迎　詣於普通門外未時入城兩使良久駐轎觀門前彩棚已而入立大廳迎慰使蘇世讓及觀察使守令等分東西行迎　詔禮畢兩使坐大廳遠接使以下一行人員行揖禮通事洪謙自京下來請謁兩使各行拜禮出兩使俱往箕子廟導者誤從文廟以入兩使曰便可拜謁遂四拜就聖殿歷觀塑像謂譯官曰汝　國崇尚文教廟貌整肅我等不勝嘉歎又詣箕子廟四拜進看位版讀庭中石碑上使曰好文章又詣檀君廟就檀君東明王位版前各行揖禮而出登練光亭挹灝樓風月樓遍觀詩板還抵大同館步往彩棚前觀雜像又坐館門良久觀優戲又登快哉亭坐話移時初昏方就房令退行迎慰宴於明朝副使在安定館臨發以所持扇子授門子門子聞失速

二十八日朝陰午雨兩使發行至雲巖院下轎若將暫歇忽促駕而出至肅寧館招遠接使同飯飯已登樓眺覽遂發行乘昏至安定館初更行宿所宴行酒再次而罷上使謂李和宗曰自肅川至此何無腰擧答曰本來無有常用帳幕供晝點而已上使曰自此抵平壤又無腰擧答曰中路有斧山院當進茶啖於右院

二十九晴辰時兩使坐大廳招遠接使共飯遂發行至斧山院招遠接使共茶啖令李和宗傳語曰今日到城內行迎 詔禮後欲拜箕子墓及文廟檀君廟仍登風月樓練光亭和宗答曰箕子墓在城外既入城則當更出城將十餘里兩使曰然則箕子墓待回來當歷拜云云行未到城十里平壤人設綵棚於兩車在兩使轎前而行優人隨車後而戲觀察使

此禮當 啓殿下處之兩使令退行迎慰宴於明日

二十七日雨在安州設迎慰宴于大廳兩使出坐遠接使與迎慰使入行禮各就坐用女樂一廵行酒而罷兩使欲冒雨發行遠接使進稟曰雨勢如此前路泥濘有甚前日敢請停行兩使曰雨若不止則當留歇若少霽則便當起身夕行留日宴々畢遠接使就兩使前令李和宗告曰國王逐日下書戒勑支供之事甚慮有差失惶恐無地 國王爲 朝廷敬大人無不用極但平時不能用酒於拜大人交接之時深恐誠意難露也兩使曰 國王祗受 詔勑故不用酒乎遠接使答曰非特此也天性不能用酒上使令李和宗語遠接使曰陪人白壽千欲帶去講書須限三兩日隨我云々即令給馬以隨之

饌初更還館副使頭目指揮田禄以橫子未遑將差使負憑川郎
守鄭允誠捽衣以詰之遠接使聞之令譯官輩語之曰此乃守土官
負惟老爹尚不肯如此加詬況汝以頭目而乃爾必須白于 天使
頭目高嵩輩謝曰彼實不知事體而妄作矣若白于 天使則
連累者必多幸乞饒他兩使招李和宗語曰汝國儒生例不迎
詔和宗對曰國俗京外儒生在學宮讀書而已非如中國隨班叅
禮所以不令迎 詔耳兩使曰儒生若不迎 詔唐學士何以有贈
定州儒生之詩乎和宗曰唐 詔使回到定州聚集儒生試觀其
周旋非因迎 詔而見也兩使曰儒生本守禮義安可廢迎 詔
大禮乎今後并令儒生迎 詔事傳語判書遠接使答曰舊無

語遠接使曰大明皇帝之語來到東國誠爲慶幸宜使大小臣民聳
觀慎勿呵止安州牧使及出站差使員等皆集江邊迎　詔即下船至
安興館迎慰使尹安仁及觀察使李龜齡各差使員等分東西拜
詔畢次受私禮即向百祥樓稱嘆江上之勝上使曰我地方亦有如此
勝景今見之不覺完然〻島遠水濶殊不及此我等續　詔拜
國王後當寫樓額宜令刻板以掛回程之日欲極其遊賞而去又令射
官射貫革一巡而罷上使見陪人白壽千頗悟問曰頗讀書乎答曰
只讀大學兩使令誦序及大文乃問曰讀書兒何故充此役乎譯官
答曰本是差役人而自能讀書也兩使大加嘆奬曰役人尚知讀書始
信東方家讀書戶禮義也又招譯官醫員令誦大學章句賞與箱

行已時到敵愾亭上使問亭名以敵愾對上使曰景物與亭名不相
合副使曰老爹宜命之仍招遠接使共坐曰今日欲觀打魚遠接使
即令漁人棹小艇橫網於江時厨中適有生鮒魚潛置艇上忽包網
以出似若新捉之狀兩使大喜親自下階而觀濡沫騰跳急取水盆
置魚其中而分其半付諸厨人午飯後兩使步上樓船招遠接使共
坐談謔頗洽上使曰此亭臨岸而構擅此一江烟浪宜以控江名之且
有朝拱　國王之意吾當書額遠接使謝曰僻陋山川多得佳名豈
非厚幸中流遠接使勸酒至八九巡舟子自遠岸網魚以來兩使欣
然甚樂未時到清川江又招遠接使共坐船上遠接使又令州人網魚
若博川江之為兩使懽甚行數巡酒而罷兩使見江邊有禁觀光者

語以請酒一語從今日始學華甚遠接使執盞進前以華語說請酒之語上使笑曰學得正是遠接使請曰欲令一行都監官獻一盃于兩使大人只恐尊威未敢開口耳兩使許之洪春卿遞酒上使曰汝有才華儆官宜早朴忠元遞酒上使曰青年好才 國王必喜遠接使又使設小華令射官張炸射之皆十中七八兩使又出前檻觀之遠接使請兩使曰此亭僻陋舊無名號今值兩大人駐節若賜之名豈非溪山之有所遭遇乎上使許諾

二十六日晴兩使出坐大廳遠接使行揖禮共坐朝飯上使曰昨日所屬亭名異老爹以齋山命之矣副使曰宜受龍其老爹文章于上使曰吾兩人中當叙名亭之義京來白牌還繳兩使見之即付頭目兩使嵗

有之上使曰欲早到嘉山觀射申時至嘉平館兩使俱以便服上東軒
後亭子急請遠接使曰帶射官來遠接使即入揖就坐令本道抄
送射官等十八員以此作耦兩射張一百七十步貫革各腰十矢遞
射三巡兩使就坐前楹以觀夕親較畫數多少起立卓面前以次賞酒
嘉歎不已遠接使以義州軍官徐慶千為家人曾告兩使徐之始射
兩使相顧稱賛射畢謂判書曰判書家人射之最好吾知此人必已
捷武舉遠接使答曰果中武舉近因革職隨我而來矣兩使又謂曹
世鳳曰汝之父子俱善射可賞蓋世鳳之子彥弼亦在射官中故也
遠接使請觀頭目等射才兩使曰日已暮矣姑待後日可也設宿所
宴酒半兩使笑曰我等逐日學得本國方音數語判書亦須學華

矣兩使同坐東軒點閱頭目曰高嵩家人何以來乎 似欲治問馭觀
差批而止上使以高嵩竊軒中蠟燭門子三名於窓隙窺覘各杖
四五板子
二十五日晴 辰時兩使發行到納清亭覽懸板訖副使指亭額納清
亭三字曰筆法不好 龔老爹善寫大字盍請改書乎俄而招遠
接使共午飯遠接使請于兩使曰此地埋沒不知其幾何年而幸見
賞於唐史兩老爹既與名亭又為作記使此溪山輝映於一方今
者復遇兩老爹奉 詔來過若賜改寫亭額豈非茲地之殼
輝乎敢以是請上使曰書字作詩俱非吾所能當囑吳老爹副
之飯訖遠接使再三進酒上使曰判書帶來家人有能射者乎答曰

令李和宗告兩使曰故事設享禮於此城例必用樂敢告兩使答
曰所謂樂爲何樂無乃婦人乎和宗曰果女樂也兩使相顧曰此不可用
遠接使迎慰使更請曰 殿下別遣内臣設享若不用樂禮不能
全以是敢瀆兩使曰在前 詔使亦或用焉兩使曰 殿下之意如是
我等欲强勉從之用諸妓筵而罷可也於是陳女樂遠接使迎慰
使各再行酒而罷上使問遠接使曰 貴國科擧例於子午卯酉
年試取云而前日又何云己巳年出身乎遠接使答曰 國俗非式
年取人謂之別試上使曰何謂別試乎遠接使答曰 國家偶有慶事
而取人矣上使曰只將國學儒生試取乎遠接使答曰四方儒生都會
試取耳上使曰永樂年間河先生膺此段別科 貴國必倣此規

拜 詔後兩使各就房小歇出坐大廳遠接使與迎慰使入行禮
問禮官就稟儀註兩使曰自城門距 王府幾里自迎 詔處
距城門幾里問禮官答曰自 王府至城門八九里自城門至郊外四五
里上使曰何不於儀註內并錄而來茶禮儀註間亦有差失然此
則不甚緊關不須故也但五拜三叩頭天下通行之禮今儀註內何無此
條問禮官往復論辨兩使曰前此 詔使皆自差失不必援引以
爲例也汝雖言 洪武禮制其時豈有 誕生 皇子頒慶外國之儀乎
我等來時過廣寧適九廟告成赦文來三堂亦於郊外行五拜
三叩頭之禮安可以中國通行之禮而獨不行於東國乎汝速回去
稟 殿下改其儀註而來初昏設迎慰宴行茶禮後遠接使迎慰使

宗傳語於遠接使曰自義州抵王々京沿途古跡山川之名及王京

各衙門該掌及品級一々寫來即依所言畧寫梗槩以給之副使

封書冊約十五六卷仍作公文付林畔館轉送于湯站

二十四日晴辰時兩使會坐大廳朝飯訖招遠接使行揖禮發行未七八

里乘馬又行十餘里至同盧河北見途邊巖石兩使俱下馬上巖

眺望還乘轎到雲興館招遠接使共飯令李和宗傳語曰判書儀容

禮度我等嘉尚但語音不同可歎史先生嘗謂我等曰朝鮮　君臣

禮容可觀但語音獨異云今果然矣兩使過孝女旌門下轎手摩碑

石看其刻畫申時至定州々官及出站差使員等迎　詣于五里

程既到館別迎慰使右承旨金亶虖守令等分東西班 迎慰使立東班 守令等立西班

時有太監來 頒誥命上使曰太監何得奉 誥命以來昌曰 王京
能解華語者幾人答曰多有上使曰然則明年 詔使之來可勾
答應矣又問曰徐學士 皇華集何獨無乎答曰其時所作不多
故不編集耳只有數篇掛在雲興館壁上上使又問曰前年進
賀冬至宰相其名為誰答曰趙仁奎上使曰去冬我與吏先生道共
觀于朝耳酒再行兩使欲罷宴遠接使出立卓外請更進一盃兩使
許之宴罷兩使出坐卓外問譯官曰判書何不由前庭而去答曰兩位
老爹在座惶恐經從堂後還去耳兩使曰可謂合禮又問李和宗曰
判書
亦知我輩懽喜乎答曰豈不知之但常以失儀為懼日甚一日耳兩使
曰判書為人厚重且知禮儀吾兩人共喜耳 汝須以此語之又令李和

答曰舊年高倭或來興敗於邊其後以無禮絕不相通上使曰琉球國人准來此地乎答曰未也申時到林畔館館前有觀光人臨路聚集者喧官令皂隷捽髮呵禁上使指李和宗曰彼衣皂者何故打人耶答曰無識之徒臨壓路上似涉不敬故禁止耳上使曰此不妨也速諭判書勿復禁止任令縱觀遠接使令李和宗稟上使曰 朝廷已封太子乎答曰此事固從所當問時未封耳我等到遼東聞文武百官請封太子 皇帝以太早不聽然今年不封則明年定封矣 詔使亦必來也酉時設宿所宴酒一行副使如廁上使問李和宗曰 國王即位想已十四五年答曰已歷三十年矣上使曰唐太史之來不在辛巳年乎答曰唐使乃須登極 詔耳 國王之即位在於丙寅年其

知上使於轎上誤墮一卷書乃寫本　皇華集也問禮官所呈儀註亦常於轎內披覽午時到車輦館兩使下轎直至盤松下以手摩撫曰此所謂盤松乎仍步入館中坐於大廳問李和宗曰箕子墓風月樓葱秀山在於何處答曰箕子墓風月樓在平壤府距此六日程也葱秀山在黃海道平山府上使又問曰本國有襲職之制乎和宗答曰有武功者襲職文官雖通顯無此法上使曰然則大官之子終不敘官職耶答曰若才器可用則詮書甄拔用之耳畫點後發行於中路上使招李和宗問曰貴國東西南北接連何地方答曰北連建州東南際海西抵鴨綠江上使曰東南海上接何地方答曰有日本國上使曰亦有繼來者乎

魚令取全體以看曰欲見其生者凡酬酢之時 天使既飲則
主人側手下擧上清果盤以勸主人則無此禮是日兩使令進果盤
於遠接使遠接使辭不敢當兩使曰我等之意如此願勿讓
也上使又指頭目崔忠曰唐太史之來汝亦隨來矣太史待
本國宰相亦如我乎此是 本國重臣只恐待之有失也崔忠
曰太史之待宰相正如老爹宴罷兩使呼李和宗語曰我等甚
喜判書文雅云是日開宴之始兩使取花柄細看良久不揷似
疑累進一花者故也
二十三日晴辰時兩使與遠接使會大廳同朝飯發行到東林城
上使指李和宗問曰此城何名答曰東林故城也世代已遠不能詳

暫駐行旌以俟明日快晴兩使許諾似有喜色遠接使仍
問曰小邦敬重　詔命頒宣之日例必擇吉敢以故事稟焉兩
使答曰此事正好當從本國所爲但太遠則不可留連太近則
恐阻雨水不及也預卜日期來告遠接使答曰遠近當不過隔
一兩日耳又問　勅書兩道之意及　欽賜有無上使曰　賜本
國只　詔書一道耳　勅書二道內一道則爲我輩防護之事二
道則我等　奏准謄黃也今次　大慶誕告海內朝廷以
本國恪謹職貢至誠無二特令諭告比內諸侯無異但無　欽賜
物件耳午後設留日宴兩使出坐與遠接使同飯兩使拱手曰
今日既承請留又設盛禮多謝〻〻酒半兩使見席中有切文

可留況春天多雨明日陰晴亦難預知兩使從索油紙先裹
詔勅次裹節鉞等物冒雨發行行十餘里兩歇兩使下轎
乘平轎至所串館點心初昏到良策館即設宿所宴兩使
出坐大廳行茶禮訖與遠接使同夕飯只行酒一巡而罷兩使
待判書行禮甚尊是日朝在義順館時帶來門子一人離側杖
其臀又於是夕杖其不謹門子三人
二十二日大風雨兩使出坐大廳同朝飯遠接使欲入行禮兩使止之曰
我等方以便服坐之不可以見冠帶之人飯訖改服出立遠接
使入謁令李和宗告曰今日前路尚遠又雨濕不得燃炬必致迷
路且本國之人未慣擔持若行泥路不無墜落撞扛之虞請

二十一日兩迎慰使吏稟衣服事副使曰此雖厚意在我不當受也
又稟曰　殿下所送衣服頭目乞聽給與答曰俟面拜　殿下然
後商量處之問禮官任彌亨吏稟儀註可否兩使答曰當到
新安館言之此先生以待上使就副使房曰今早下雨雖不得發
行不須與判書相會巳時兩使會坐東軒朝飯急招李和宗曰
我等當即發行其語諸判書時雨勢不止路甚泥濘遠接使
就上使房欲達停行之意上使遽出坐大廳副使亦來同坐遠
接使就前行揖仍語曰今既日晚雨又不絕前路脩遠轎軍亦
恐蹉跌以此皇恐上使曰判書請留主人之禮然也我等爲王事
不可留滯判書奉　殿下敬客之意在而我等已知之然決不

白書來遠接使即令寫驛站里數及一行人並一路名差使員等官
職姓名呈于兩使前上使語李和宗曰朝廷深愛　本國故特以
大慶事來頒爾李和宗答曰　朝廷撫恤我國一國臣民感戴
皇恩因問安南國亦頒下　詔否上使曰未也只頒　詔於十三布政
司南京及　本國耳李和宗又問曰今既有　詔又有兩　勅旨何
也上使答曰　勅則非關汝　國係於我輩之句當耳和宗又問曰
今次有　欽賜否上使曰欽賜事竢後日當與大官面說云云　迎
慰使以京來衣服等物分給頭目等頭目等皆不受曰當稟
老爹處之令不可擅受云夜設頭目宴享於中門外一應天使宴享處例有頭目宴後皆倣此

郎官亦文職也方宴時兩使曰本國素守禮義我等曾已飽聞
故一切禮文不須相問上使見馳駱粥問此冷耶熱耶通事答
曰此則冷粥亦有熱粥上使曰吏令湯來即湯以進兩使俱飲
幾盡一椀兩使各就房迎慰使令通事分呈衣服單字上使
覽而笑曰我不與　國王相面而何爲受禮且凡禮單例用紅
紙以寫又以紅紙作外套禮也判尹因爲知禮之官何用白紙
寫來乎李和宗答曰單用紅紙　本國古無此俗兩使曰明日
當吏酌量而說之是日兩使越江時回送樂工十九名旣到義
州義順館用朱筆又其批文內名字兩使指通事曰明日當
宿何館答曰當宿良策館兩使曰自此距王京里數詰名明

使前完盃禮如上使儀次遠接使行酒如迎慰使行酒禮次進
大膳迎慰使遠接使再行酒禮如初儀兩使曰夜深又醉止酒
可也罷宴迎慰使告辭上使曰今日盛禮既見 國王之誠意我等
俱是行客此卓面之物實無用處令州官收之可也遂移交倚坐
於中央曰我等在此時可速撤去遠接使令通事稟曰此宴餘
之物給與從者兩使曰我帶來之人皆有宴禮然熟饌則容
可給也如生物油果俱不可與他兩使從容談話因問通事
曰吳判尹何年出身答曰甲子年出身又問鄭判書何年出
身答曰己巳年出身又問判尹判書職品高下答曰俱是正二品
平安都事安璘告辭 上使曰都事為何官答曰本道觀察使之

使飮訖迎慰使助進果盤又就樽所酌酒進副使前行酒如右
各就坐次進湯迎慰使出就樽所酌酒揖進上使上使答揖執盞
與迎慰使揖舉盞與副使半揖又與遠接使半揖與迎慰使揖
飮訖授盞如初儀助進果盤迎慰使又就樽所酌酒連進上使前
上使揖禮如初飮訖助進果盤上使令執事酌酒來揖與迎慰
使迎慰使答揖執盞與上使揖上使答揖又與副使揖副使答
揖還與上使揖上使答揖迎慰使飮訖迎慰使就樽所酌酒
副使前行禮如上使前儀又就樽所酌酒上使前揖進完盞上使
答揖執盞又與迎慰使揖迎慰使答揖上使飮訖授虛盞于迎
慰使迎慰使受虛盞傳授執事與上使揖果盤助進又於副

大廳北壁遠接使迎慰使就兩使前各行揖禮兩使起立答揖
遠接使迎慰使就西壁立兩使擧手請坐遠接使迎慰使坐
交倚行茶禮訖迎慰使呈庭排物膳單宣兩使覽訖曰此物
國不當受但於此足見賢王誠意云云先進花次進小膳次進揮巾
次進湯次進果盤迎慰使出就樽所酌宣慰酒進上使前揖上
使答揖上使執盞與迎慰使揖擧盞與副使半揖又與遠接使
擧手半揖還與迎慰使揖迎慰使答揖上使不許迎慰使執盞
飮訖授虛盞于迎慰使迎慰使受虛盞傳授執事與上使相揖
果盤助進上使食訖與迎慰使拱手迎慰使亦拱手又詣樽所酌
酒進上使前揖上使答揖上使執盞與迎慰使揖迎慰使答揖上

仍於　闕牌左右相向而立遠接使迎慰使從事官通事醫[illegible]
入於東庭各官差使員入於西庭行四拜上香又行四拜禮畢
奉　詔勅出安于大廳後幕次兩使至幕次觀安　詔後仍[illegible]
往東軒又自東軒往西軒副使從上使于大廳相揖各就東
西上房良久兩使各着冠帶出坐大廳別通事先入行再拜
禮兩使坐椅子只拱手答禮別通事分立東西遠接使入各行
再拜迎慰使亦入行再拜兩使起立答揖次從事官次醫員[illegible]
各務差使員次問禮官各行再拜兩使皆坐只拱手答揖問禮
官呈儀註而出兩使還就東軒以便服遍覽前人所題懸板今[illegible]
人先設卓面於大廳通事告迎慰宴之禮兩使又着冠帶[illegible]

嘉靖十六年二月 日

二十日雨未時雨 天使到鴨綠江北岸宴廳令遼東通事高嵩

傳呼曰李通事和宗速將紙筆過江來遠接使聞之令譯學訓

導顔伯衡馳進未幾 天使越江到此邊宴廳問顔伯衡曰李和

宗何不來乎遠接使亦逆于何處顔伯衡答曰遠接使及通事在

員等例在義順館迎 詔故今不敢來矣義州牧使張彥良入

行再拜兩使坐交倚不答禮仍行茶禮令彥良進酒連三盃

申時乘本國氈轎至五里程牧使及差使員等以朝服鞠躬

詔遂前導以行遠接使迎慰使從事官通事醫員等大門外

祗迎兩使入中門階下下轎隨 詔勅而入親奉 詔勅置[illegible]

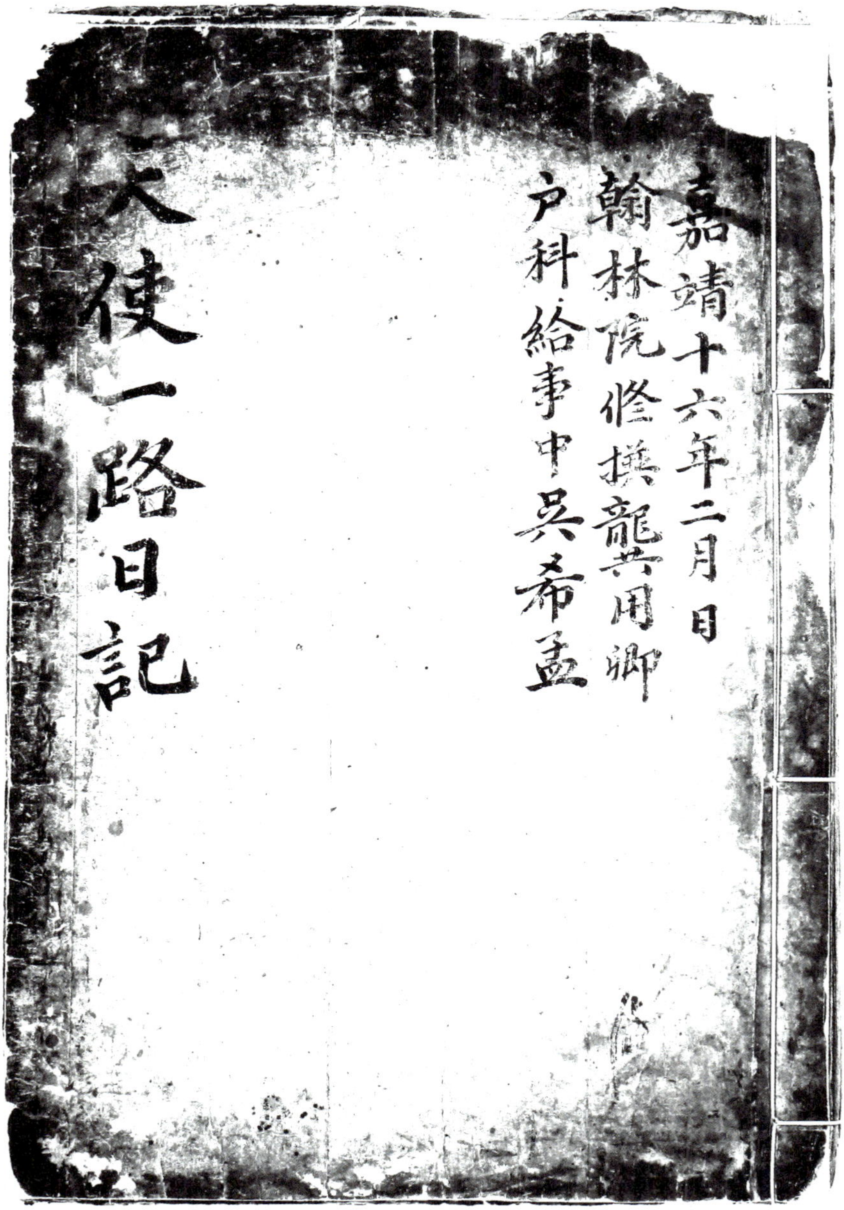

嘉靖十六年二月日

翰林院修撰龔用卿

户科給事中吳希孟

天使一路日記